AF010

MASSIMILIANO AFIERO

AXIS FORCES
10

WW2 AXIS
FORCES

The Axis Forces 010 - First edition June 2019 by Luca Cristini Editor for the brand Soldiershop
Cover & Art Design by soldiershop factory. ISBN code: 978-88-93274692

The Axis Forces number 10 – May 2019

Direction and editing
Via San Giorgio, 11 – 80021 AFRAGOLA (NA) -ITALY

Managing and Chief Editor: Massimiliano Afiero
Email: maxafiero@libero.it - **Website**: www.maxafiero.it

Contributors
Tomasz Borowski, Stefano Canavassi, Carlos Caballero Jurado, Rene Chavez, Carlo Cucut, Daniel Fanni, Dmitry Frolov, Antonio Guerra, John B. Köser, Lars Larsen, Christophe Leguérandais, Eduardo M. Gil Martínez, Peter Mooney, Péter Mujzer, Ken Niewiarowicz, Erik Norling, Raphael Riccio, Marc Rikmenspoel, Charles Trang, Cesare Veronesi, Sergio Volpe

Editorial

After the February issue, this new issue, the tenth, comes out in May. We are counting on eliminating this one-month delay in normal quarterly programming as early as the next issue, which should come out in July or at most with the October issue. In any case, despite all the difficulties, our historical research work continues, always hoping to meet your interest. We are always trying to deal with new and unpublished topics, as far as possible of course and we are always looking for new collaborators to be able to deal with new topics on Axis forces in the Second World War. We are happy to accept your work (in digital format of course to our email address) and we promise you that we will take everything and everyone into consideration, while respecting the quality level of our magazine. We thank everyone for their cooperation. Let's now analyze the contents of this new issue of the magazine. We begin with a long and exhaustive article on the employment of Totenkopf Division on the Ukrainian front in the summer of 1943, rich as always with numerous photos, following the biography of Otto Kumm, one of the most known and decorated officers of Waffen-SS. It continues with the fourth and last part of the article dedicated to the Barbarigo battalion on the Anzio front and with a new excerpt from the new book by Tomasz Borowski on the final combat actions of the French volunteers of the Charlemagne. We close with the first part of a new study dedicated to the campaign in North Africa, a work that will later be integrated into a book (which will be published both in Italian and in English), which we hope will soon see the light. Happy reading to everyone and see you in the next issue.

Massimiliano Afiero

Contents

in World War Two 1939-1945

The Totenkopf Division on the Ukrainian Front, August 1943
by Massimiliano Afiero

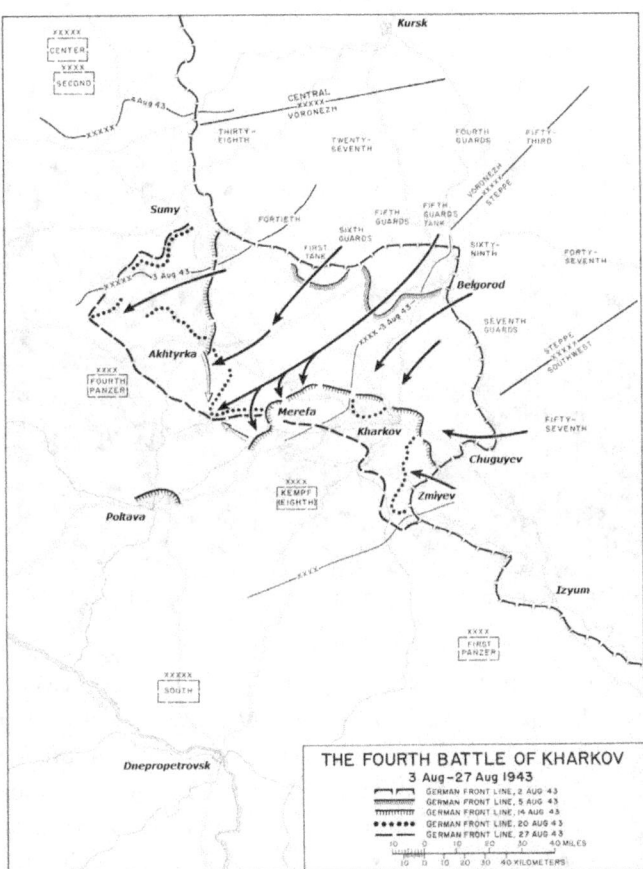

The Soviet offensive between August 2-27, 1943.

Soviet tanks and infantry in the attack, August 1943.

On August 1, 1943, while fighting was still in progress on the Mius front, the *II.SS-Pz.Korps* headquarters received orders to prepare for withdrawal of the *Das Reich*, the *Totenkopf* and *3.Panzer-Division*, in order to shift them as quickly as possible to the Kharkov area. This was because strong Soviet troop concentrations had been spotted in the area between Bjelgorod and Tomarowka, which had assembled there in the matter of a few days. And thus, across a front barely forty kilometers wide, the Voronezh Front had a total of four armies: the 5th Guards, the 6th Guards, the 1st Tank and the 5th Guards Tank. On August 1, the last two of these armies had 542 and 503 tanks, respectively. The Soviets had been able to reorganize their tank forces in less than fifteen days and this proved von Manstein to be right, as he had requested permission to continue the offensive against the southern flank of the Kursk salient in order to wipe out those two armies once and for all.

Operation Rumyantsev

On August 3, 1943, the Soviets launched a new offensive, Operation *Polkovodets Rumyantsev*; the forces of the Voronezh Front attacked between Bjelgorod and Tomarowka, and those of the Steppe Front, to the east of the Donetz. The

LII.Armee-Korps, with the *332.Inf.Div.* and the *167.Inf.Div.* on the front line and with the *6.* and *19.Pz.Div.* in reserve, found itself facing the main thrust of the Soviet attack. After having been subjected to a massive artillery bombardment, the two infantry divisions were overwhelmed by the enemy assault, while the two armored divisions were able to slow down the Soviet advance for only a few hours.

A *PzKpfw.III* of *I./SS-Pz.Rgt.3* crossing a river along with army troops (*Charles Trang*).

SS troops on the march, August 1943.

The German front was broken through and a dangerous gap was opened between *4.Panzerarmee* and *Armee-Abteilung Kempf*. On 5 August, Bjelgorod was taken by forces of the Voronezh Front and three other Soviet armies went on the attack west of Tomarowka, forcing the German troops into a general retreat.

The clashes west of Kharkov

On August 5, the *3.Pz.Div.* and the Das Reich reached the Kharkov sector. According to German plans, the *III.Pz.Korps* was to be committed to close the breach and make contact with the *XXIV.Pz.Korps*, which was to attack from west to east. When the *Totenkopf*, which had already seen hard fighting for the capture of Hill 213.9, received its marching orders, it was in such a disastrous state that its men thought that they would surely be sent back to Germany. On August 7, the Soviets seized Bogoduchoff, where they captured intact immense stores of fuel and ammunition of *Armee-Abteilung Kempf*. From there they continued on to the southwest, to the other side of the Merla River. At Gorlowka, the tracked elements of the *Totenkopf* were loaded aboard trains, while the wheeled vehicles proceeded by road. Soviet aviation became increasingly present as the convoys approached closer to Kharkov. In the Staritowskaja area, Soviet artillery shelled the eastern bank of the Donetz, forcing the convoys to make a wide detour. The *Totenkopf* thus took three days to cover the three hundred kilometers that separated it from Merefa.

A *Befehlspanzer III* of II./SS-Pz.Rgt.3 north of Walki (*Charles Trang*).

An *SdKfz.10* of the *Totenkopf* moving towards Kharkov.

The division, which was the last *III.Pz.Korps* unit to reach the Kharkov area, was ordered to close the forty-kilometer gap that separated *Armee-Abteilung Kempf* from *4.Panzerarmee*, between Udarnyj and Kolontajew. On August 8, the bulk of the division assembled between Ogulzy and Walki. The first units of the *Totenkopf* to reach the sector along the Mertschik River immediately established positions along a line that ran from Suchoj to Mertschik, where the *SS-Rgt."TE"* was deployed, to the area south of the Mertschik, where the *SS-Rgt."T"* was deployed on both sides of Alexandrowka. On the left flank, the reconnaissance group, led by *SS-Stubaf.* Krauth, defended a twenty-kilometer front between Scharowka and Krasnokutsk. Meanwhile, the tracked elements were arriving piecemeal. The following day, the *Totenkopf* extended its sector further to the west, but due to the lack of vehicles, it was forced to set up isolated strongpoints. Towards evening, the division reported the following vehicles available: fourteen *PzKpfw III*, twenty-seven *PzKpfw IV*, and eleven *StuG III*.

Closeup of a *Befehlspanzer III* turret (*Charles Trang*).

A *Totenkopf* NCO.

Totenkopf scouts in an area west of Kharkov.

During the night of August 9-10, the Soviets attacked and crossed the Mertschik and invested the village of Kowjagi, thus threatening the rear of the *Totenkopf*. Elements of *I./SS-Pz.Rgt.3* that were at Walki were quickly shifted to that area. Their commander, *SS-Ostuf.* Burgschulte, was decapitated by a direct hit by an enemy artillery round. Shortly after, the Soviet troops were pushed back to the north. What was left of the battalion was then reorganized: two combat groups were formed, the *1.Kampfgruppe*, led by *SS-Ostuf.* Riefkogel, consisted of the remnants of *1.* and *2.Kp.* The *2.Kampfgruppe*, led by *SS-Ostuf.* Altermüller, consisted of the other elements of the battalion. *SS-Ostuf.* Riefkogel was wounded in the head and Altermüller was killed a few hours later during an accidental bombing by the *Luftwaffe*. The two *Kampfgruppen* were then amalgamated and the new combat group was put under command of the battalion's orderly, *SS-Ostuf.* Herbatscheck.

A Soviet *Matilda* tank knocked out south of Merla (*Charles Trang Collection*).

A *Totenkopf* defensive position with an *MG-34*.

A Soviet soldier armed with a *PPSh*.

On the Mertschik front

Meanwhile, the Soviets concentrated fresh troops in the area south of the Merla River. Around 15:15, those forces attacked the left flank of the '*Eicke*' Regiment. Further to the west, other enemy units threatened to seize a bridge over the Mertschik near the village of Murafa. Accompanied by Soviet infantrymen, some tanks surprised the engineer unit that was assigned to blow the bridge. A fault in the electrical detonator prevented the SS engineers from destroying the bridge, just as the first Soviet soldiers began to cross it. Some *Totenkopf* recon troops had to go into action to throw back the enemy infantry and to allow one of the engineers to repair the ignition charge. In the end, the bridge was blown into the air. But soon after, covered by fire from *T-34* tanks on the northern bank, Soviet infantry tried to cross the river, making their way over the ruins of the destroyed bridge. Dozens of men were killed by small arms fire from the SS troops. However, further waves of infantry attacked, and the Soviets finally managed to establish a bridgehead on the southern bank of the Mertschik. It was a real disaster for the *Totenkopf* troops. During the night of August 10-11, the situation continued to be worrisome, when the Soviets attacked to the south from their bridgehead at Alexandrowka. The attack was rebuffed, but the SS troops opted to withdraw to Walki to regroup. At the same time, a Soviet tank formation attacked the position at Wyssokopolje.

SS grenadiers moving from their positions to counterattack.

Pioneer of the *SS-Pi.Btl.3*.

Final orders for a *Tiger* tank commander.

Attacking Soviet infantry and an anti-tank gun.

A company from *SS-Pz.Rgt.3* was sent to head it off. During the fighting that ensued, numerous T-34 tanks were knocked out and the remaining Soviet troops chose to withdraw. In the morning, fresh enemy troops arrived south of the Mertschik and which attacked and easily broke through the *Totenkopf* lines south of Alexandrowka. The division was ordered by *III.Pz.Korps* to re-establish the situation at all costs. Some grenadiers, supported by panzers and assault guns, were thrown into a counterattack. Around noon, after heavy fighting, the SS troops were able to secure the southern bank of the Mertschik between Alexandrowka and Scharowka. To the southwest, *SS-Pi.-Btl.'T'* recaptured Wyssokopolje, where many tanks were knocked out at close range. The Soviets had also crossed the Mertschik at Murafa and headed to the south, forcing the *Totenkopf* reconnaissance group to withdraw its left wing to Katschalowka. At the same time, other enemy tank formations continued to push from the Mertschik sector towards Perekop. Beginning at 1600, six Tigers under *SS-Ustuf*. Quade launched a counterattack towards Kolomak and during the night Tschutowo was captured. At the end of the day, the division found itself defending a fifty kilometer front running from Maximowka in the east and Krasnokutsk to the west.

A German tank formation during an attack, Summer 1943.

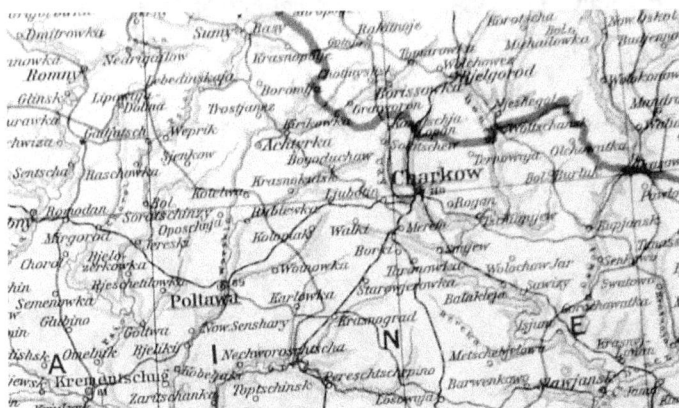

The area northwest of Kharkov.

An assault gun in a field of sunflowers, August 1943.

The *Totenkopf* had been able to block the Soviet 1st Tank Army offensive, inflicting heavy damage on it and, despite being severely tested itself, was involved in the *III.Pz.Korps* counterattack which was scheduled for the following day. With it, the German command sought to try to destroy the Soviet tank forces that had managed to break through to the south. Those forces had not yet been joined by the rifle divisions, which were still engaged in fighting on the flanks of the breakthrough. The *III.Pz.Korps* plan called for an attack on two parallel axes, with the *Das Reich* heading towards Bogoduchoff tasked with cutting the Soviet 6th Tank Corps lines of communication and the Totenkopf advancing towards Murafa to cut off Soviet units which had ventured south of the Mertschik. *SS-Pz.Rgt.3* reported that it was down to thirty-nine operational panzers, to which could be added another thirteen *Tiger* tanks of *s.Pz.Abt.503*, the Tiger heavy battalion, that had been attached to the division. On August 12, the Soviets were the first to attack: at 0345, about twenty tanks penetrated the *Totenkopf* lines east of Alexandrowka.

A *Totenkopf MG-34* on a tripod, August 1943.

A column of Tiger tanks.

They were thrown back by the Tigers of *9.(s.)Kp./SS-Pz.Rgt.3*. In the early afternoon, the Tigers supported the *'Eicke'* Regiment in its attack against Pawlowo. During the attack, around 1700, the Tigers ran up against an anti-tank front. *SS-Uscha.* Fein's Tiger, *'913'*, was hit by an American-origin 90 mm anti-tank gun and caught fire.

Photos of *SS-Uscha.* Fein's *Tiger '913'*, still burning, August 1943.

A Soviet T-34 tank and infantry entering a village.

The entire crew was killed. The loader, Franz Hofer, who had been pulled out of the tank still alive, died soon after from the serious wounds he had sustained. Another four Tigers suffered direct hits from the Soviet anti-tank guns. At the end of the fighting, the company counted seven killed. The last operational Tiger, belonging to *SS-Ustuf.* Heinz Quade, following massive *Nebelwerfer* fire, supported the breakthrough of the enemy anti-tank screen and captured Hill 195.1, which was occupied at 18:45. Despite having suffered two frontal hits, Quade's tank was not damaged. On the division's left flank the Soviets were luckier; a tank corps and a rifle division crossed the Merla river between Krasnokutsk and Kolantejew, pushing south, southeast and east. At 8:45, *III.Pz.Korps* itself went on the attack. At the same time the *Das Reich*, supported by the *'Eicke'* Regiment, crossed the Suchoj Mertschik from the Skossogorowka-Sachny area.

Officers of *13.(I.G.)/SS-Pz.Gr.Rgt.5 'T'*: from the left, *SS-Uscha.* Beck, *SS-Ostuf.* Ahnhorst, company commander, and *SS-Hstuf.* Restorff.

A *Totenkopf* defensive mortar emplacement.

Despite their numerical superiority, the Soviets were overrun. On the other side, the SS troops attacked Alexandrowka, capturing around ten trucks and five anti-tank guns. But soon after, the Soviets tried to retake the place; during the fighting that ensued they lost twenty-two tanks, most of which were knocked out by the assault guns of *SS-StuG.Abt. 'Totenkopf'*. Further to the east, *Das Reich* troops inflicted heavy losses on the 5th Guards Tank Army, but were unable to seize Bogoduchoff, due mainly to the presence of infantry units of the 32nd Rifle Corps south of the city.

A *T-34* in an attack, August 1943.

A battle of annihilation

During the night between 12 and 13 August, the 1st Guards Tank Army attacked south of the Merla, towards Katschalowka. Under strong enemy pressure, *SS-P.Aufkl.-Abt.* 'T' was forced to abandon that location around 0530. Soviet troops were thus able to threaten Kolomak and Kostantinowka. Despite the critical situation on its left wing, *III.Pz.Korps* continued its offensive to the west: the *'Eicke'* Regiment attacked as planned, towards Nikitowka. The *'Totenkopf'* Regiment followed it north of the Mertschik River. The SS troops advanced rapidly, inflicting heavy losses on the Soviet units they met along the way. Nikitowka fell into the hands of the *'Theodor Eicke'* Regiment at 1050; large quantities of supplies were seized there. On the other hand, on the left wing, the division's recon group had to withdraw in the face of an attack by two Guards rifle divisions and the 5th Guards Tank Corps. Further to the west, *4.Panzerarmee* had been able to stop the offensive in front of Achtyrka and was preparing to throw the *XXIV.Pz.Korps* into a counterattack.

SS-Standartenführer Helmuth Becker.

The Knight's Cross for Hellmuth Becker

During the fighting for the capture of Nikitowka, particularly distinguishing himself was *SS-Standartenführer* Hellmuth Becker, commander of *SS-Pz.Gren.Rgt. 'Theodor Eicke'*, who was awarded the Knight's Cross on September 7, 1943, as proposed by *SS-Brigdf.* Priess. The text of the citation states: "...*On August 13, 1943, SS-Pz.Gren.Rgt. 'Eicke' had been ordered to take Nikitowka and hills 199.8 and 197.4, situated further to the west. The location fell into SS hands around noon, but nonetheless they were unable to continue their advance because of violent fire against their flanks coming from strong field fortifications west of that location. On his own initiative, Becker then decided to bring up his reserve battalion along the route reserved for the division that was on his right in order to seize Hill 197.1, bypassing it to the north and thus opening the way from the northwest to hills 199.8 and 197.4. Thanks to his personal involvement, he achieved the capture of Hill 197.1, after which he turned southwest to attack hills 199.8 and 197.4. Those two hills ended up in his hands, thus allowing the division to continue its offensive towards the Mertschik river the following day. This led to the elimination of two rifle divisions, two tank brigades and a mechanized brigade."*

13 August 1943: Grenadiers of *III./'Theodor Eicke'* conferring with tankers of *s.Pz.Abt. 503*, prior to attacking Nikitowka.

A *Totenkopf* runner with a message to deliver.

Employment of the II.SS-Pz.Rgt.3

On August 14, shortly after midnight, the *III.Pz.Korps* prepared to attack the Soviet units that had crossed the Mertschik River. At 10:00, the division received the order to withdraw the *'Theodor Eicke'* Regiment from the front line without waiting to be relieved by troops of the *'Der Führer'* regiment of the *Das Reich*.

A formation of *PzKpfw IV* moving to attack.

On the left flank the situation continued to be very critical for the *Totenkopf* recon troops and engineers. Meanwhile, Soviet forces had taken Kolomak and south of Krasnokutsk they were able to penetrate more than thirty kilometers. Around 1500, the *'Totenkopf'* and *'Eicke'* regiments assumed positions along the Scharowka-Dergatschi road. The attack was launched at 1630, against the flank of Soviet units that were advancing southeast of the Merla River. *SS-Oscha.* Stettner relates the employment of the *II.SS-Pz.Rgt.3* during that day : *"The 5.Kompanie was engaged on the left flank. The Tigers [of s.Pz.Abt.503] were instead engaged on the right, where enemy resistance was stronger. The attack moved across the fields of sunflowers, corn and grain. After a series of hills, the ground began to slope downward. Our assault guns emerged on our left. From somewhere in a sunflower field an anti-tank gun began to fire on them. We moved out in search of the gun. We quickly found ourselves facing it. The gun crew worked feverishly to fire against us. Our driver went ahead at full speed, making the engine whine. I saw the terror on the faces of the Soviets. Then the screech of metal against metal could be heard. The anti-tank gun and its crew ended up under our tracks....*

A *PzKpfw III* moving in an attack through a field of sunflowers.

A knocked-out *T-34*, August 1943.

There were numerous exchanges of fire to our right. We made it to a field of sunflowers. A village [Sotnaja] appeared to our front. We dived into it. The inhabitants gave us to understand that the Soviets, with a dozen tanks, had left the place. We took up a position at the eastern edge of the village and fired on the Soviet infantry that was fleeing. We set off in pursuit of them. The panzers from our battalion were now on our right. We then turned to the northeast and marched in an attack formation across a valley that widened out. In the distance I spotted the buildings of a sugar factory. There, at about two thousand meters, were some enemy tanks. More kept on coming. We counted thirty, then forty. We threw ourselves against them. They disappeared in a sunflower field. We could see the sunflowers ending up under the treads of the Soviet tanks. After having left the cover of the field, they tried to turn to the left towards a woods. An order from our commander Bochmann rang in our earphones: 'Tigers and Panzer IV, *fire at will. Range 1600. Panzer III, move to the right! We have to get them in a pincer'. We moved to the right flank and attacked. The* Tiger *and* Panzer IV *tanks continued to fire against the enemy. The first columns of smoke that came from the burning T-34s rose high to the heavens. The valley echoed from the sound of the cannons and the noise of the explosions.*

A *PzKpfw III* firing on enemy positions during an attack.

We got into firing positions and engaged in combat with our Panzer III *tanks. Some of the Soviet tanks attempted to flee, but were immobilized by our concentrated fire. We continued our attack, but soon found ourselves under strong enemy anti-tank fire".*

A *Totenkopf* soldier.

A *Totenkopf* 75 mm anti-tank gun.

By the end of that day, *III.Pz.Korps* had been able to stabilize its right flank and its center. On the other hand, the Soviet troops continued to advance dangerously on its left flank, where there were not many forces to stop them. At dawn on 15 August the *Totenkopf* went on the attack towards Konstantinowka, with the aim of destroying the enemy forces that had advanced south of the Merla and the Mertschik. At 8:10 the 'Eicke' Regiment attacked Sachalin, defended by two Soviet regiments. After having abandoned their heavy weapons, around 10:00, the Soviet troops were put to flight following heavy fighting. It was not until 1115 that the day's objective, Konstantinowka, was taken by *I./SS-Pz.Rgt.3*. The bulk of the '*Totenkopf*' Regiment then pushed on as far as Slobodka, towards the Merla River. At that point the division's two grenadier regiments pivoted southeast in order to take from the rear the Soviet units that were in the Kolomak sector. Enemy resistance was nipped in the bud and the SS troops captured hundreds of prisoners. The '*Totenkopf*' Regiment was soon able to make contact with *SS-Pz.Aufkl.-Abt. 'T'* at Surdowka. In a panic, what was left of the Soviet garrison tried to escape across the fields. Completely exposed, the poor Soviet soldiers were cut down by fire from German machine guns. *I./SS-Pz.Rgt.3* later broke through the heart of the Soviet line: supported by several SPW, the *SS-Pz.Abteilung* mounted an attack at 1300, towards Kolmak and Tschutowo, quickly making contact with the enemy. An infantry position was overrun before Soviet tanks joined the action.

SS grenadiers and a *PzKpfw III Ausf J* in the area west of Kharkov, August 1943.

An *MG-34* opening fire against enemy infantry.

Stukas showed up at the right moment, destroying several enemy tanks, while the panzers themselves knocked out another four. Once this initial obstacle was overcome, *I./SS-Pz.Rgt.3* reached the outskirts of Kolomak, which was defended by a Soviet female battalion. The place fell to the SS troops following a shelling by 75 mm guns and the arrival of grenadiers riding half-tracks. The *Kampfgruppe* encountered no further resistance and reached Tschutowo early in the evening. The *Totenkopf* thus was able to surround elements of several rifle divisions and of the 6th Tank Corps in the Alexejewka-Konstantinowka-Medjaniki-Bidilo area. The SS troops closed in on Alexejewka that same evening, while *SS-Pi.-Btl. 'T'* literally cut to pieces the Soviet units that were surrounded in Wyssokopolje. The threat on the left wing of *III.Pz.Korps* was temporarily fended off, but the forty kilometer gap that separated *4.Panzerarmee* from *8.Armee* had still not been closed. During the night of August 15-16, the Soviet forces that were surrounded attempted to take advantage of darkness to break out to the northwest but were not successful and suffered heavy losses. At dawn, *SS-Rgt. 'T'*, supported by most of *SS-Pz.Rgt.3* and *SS-Pi.-Btl. 'T'*, went on the attack. The sector north of Alexejewka was cleared out around 11:00; the Soviets left more than two hundred and fifty dead on the field. Around noon, the *Totenkopf* troops regrouped and awaited new orders. In fact, after having attacked west of Nikitowka and Kowjagi between 12 and 14 August, then to the southeast towards Wyssokopolje and Konstantinowka between 15 and 16 August, the division prepared to push on to the north, towards the Merla River.

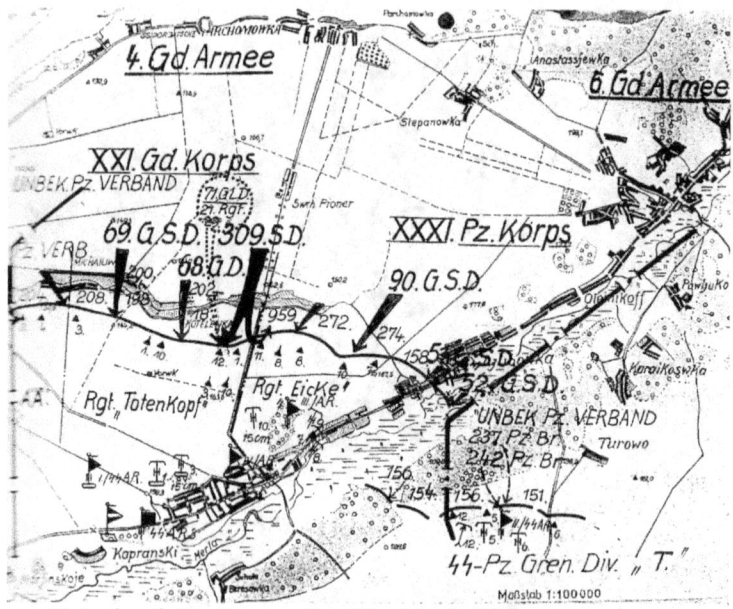

Totenkopf situation north of the Merla River, August 1943.

Totenkopf grenadiers.

A *Totenkopf* 20 mm *Flak* gun.

On the Merla River front

At around 0245 on August 17, an assault group from *6.Kp./'T'* was able to surprise Soviet troops and capture two of three bridges over the Merla at Kolantejew. The third bridge, however, was strongly defended and the SS troops suffered heavy losses, attacking across flat and marshy ground that offered no cover. Under those conditions, almost any forward movement seemed impossible, despite support by the 150 mm howitzers of *11.Batterie*. The efforts of the men of the *Totenkopf* were in vain; those who managed to make it to the opposite bank were taken under Soviet fire. The bridgehead finally had to be abandoned. On the right wing of the *Totenkopf*, the *II./'TE'* in turn attacked towards the Merla. Shortly thereafter the SS battalion was stalled in front of the village of Karaikosowka. The *I./'T'* was then sent in reinforcement, and at the same time the *III./'T'* was sent to support the *II./'T'*, south of Kolantejew. The attack by the SS grenadiers quickly broke down in the marshes and was definitively halted by heavy Soviet artillery fire. At 1800, the *'Eicke'* Regiment again attempted to cross the Merla River, this time south of Oleinikoff. However, even that attempt achieved no positive result.

A *Totenkopf* defensive position with an *MG-34*, August 1943.

Totenkopf grenadiers.

Towards evening, *Heeresgruppe Süd* confirmed the orders for the following day: *XXIV.Pz.Korps* (*4.Pz.Armee*) was to attack, moving from the area of Achtyrka towards Kotelwa to establish contact with *III.Pz.Korps* (*8.Armee*). The *Totenkopf* troops in particular had to cross the Merla River at Ljubowka and Oleinikoff. Their attack was to kick off at 1030. At the prescribed hour, the *III./'TE'* attacked towards Ljubowka, located on the banks of the Merla River. The attack was stalled again by enemy fire, with heavy losses to the SS troops. The attack by the *I./'T'* against Hill 102.7 likewise did not yield any worthwhile results. The only positive note was that during the fighting at least forty-four Soviet tanks were destroyed. The *III.Pz.Korps* issued the same orders for the following day: the *Totenkopf* was to cross the Merla and attack northwards, towards Parchomowka, to make contact with the *Grossdeutschland*. On August 19, assault groups from the *'Eicke'* and *'Totenkopf'* regiments again attempted to cross the river. It was a difficult task because the Soviets were well dug in on the hills that dominated the entire sector. At 1050, the *II./'TE'* managed to invest Oleinikoff and establish a bridgehead on the northern bank of the Merla. Reinforcing it was, however, difficult, due to Soviet artillery and mortar fire. Nonetheless, around 1530, reinforcements were able to reach the bridgehead allowing it to be expanded to the northeast.

A trench defended by *Totenkopf* troops on the Merla River front.

A *Totenkopf* soldier.

Meanwhile, the *I./'TE'* made it to the outskirts of Ljubowka. The Soviets counterattacked shortly afterwards. The SS troops again suffered heavy losses during the renewed fighting: the *1./'TE'* was wiped out within a few minutes. During the morning, *SS-Pz.Aufkl.-Abt. 'T'* also attacked, but to the southwest, along the southern bank of the Merla. Its objective was to repel the Soviet forces that were located between Rublewka and Truschanowka before heading towards the river in the direction of Kolontajew. The *1.(SPW)Kp.* attacked towards the Worskla River and at 1100, seized the bridge over the Bystraja River, located northwest of Solonizewka. The SS scouts then moved on towards Marinskoje, where the Soviets had anchored their defense. The position was captured after bitter close-quarter fighting. At that point, the SS recon troops were able to push on towards Parchomowka.

Kurt Franke with the *Ritterkreuz*.

Totenkopf grenadiers, August 1943.

The Knight's Cross for Kurt Franke

SS-Uscha. Kurt Franke particularly distinguished himself on the Merla front: leading a single rifle squad and a machine gun squad, he was able to establish a bridgehead on the Merla River, defending the position against numerous enemy attacks. As a result of his success in that latest round of fighting, Franke was awarded the Knight's Cross, officially on 3 October 1943, as *SS-Hauptscharführer und Stoßtruppführer 11./SS-Pz.Gren.Rgt.6 'Theodor Eicke'*, with the following citation, written by *SS-Stubaf.* Max Kühn, commander of the *III./'TE'*: "..On 18.8.1943, the III./SS-Pz.Gren.Rgt. 'Theodor Eicke' *was assigned the mission to establish a bridgehead on the Merla river. The battalion attacked on the western side of the Karaiskowka woods, where an intense enemy interdiction fire using all available weapons stalled the attack of the battalion's troops, who, despite all of their best efforts, took heavy losses. On 19.8.1943,* SS-Hauptscharführer *Franke was given the mission to advance with an assault unit towards Oleinikoff in order to determine the exact strength of enemy defenses along the western bank of the Merla. Franke moved across the battlefield with his assault team to the sector of the front where enemy fire was lighter. He then infiltrated along the only route possible, the long marshy canals that led to near the village from which a fair amount of fire was emanating. After having dug foxholes, Frank made the bold decision to try to enter the village. Without paying much heed to the violent enemy fire, he entered Oleinikoff at the head of his men, quickly establishing a small bridgehead on the spot. He then defended the position against numerous enemy attempts to eliminate the infiltration, which in the meantime had been reinforced and had expanded his bridgehead in the swamps to about two kilometers. With this personal decision, SS-Hauptscharführer Franke created the prerequisites for a jump-off point for SS-Pz.Gren.Rgt. 'Theodor Eicke', which during fighting that followed southeast of Achtyrka was able to establish contact with a regiment of the* Pz.Div. Grossdeutschland, *which was advancing from the northwest".*

A 20 mm *Flak 37* gun mounted on an *SdKfz. 6* half-track, August 1943.

SS scouts and an SPW armored car.

The battle continues

During the night of August 19-20, the *I./SS-Pz.Rgt.3, the I.(gep.)/'T'* and the *1.(Sfl.)Kp./SS-Pz.Jg.-Abt. 'T'* arrived to reinforce the bridgehead at Solonizewka. This strong armored group prepared to attack Kolontajew, while several patrols from the reconnaissance group attempted to make contact with troops of the *Grossdeutschland*. The *Panzerkampfgruppe*, which had been taken under heavy Soviet artillery fire which had also wounded *SS-Stubaf.* Meierdress, crossed the Merla River but ran into stiff resistance northwest of Kolantejew. At 1030, the *Totenkopf* received orders to refrain from engaging in combat in villages along the Merla sector. Only *SS-Pz.Aufkl.-Abt. 'T'* was sent to the north, towards the *XXIV.Pz,Korps*. The SS scouts quickly reached the Kolantejew-

Kotelwa road. Meanwhile, the *Grossdeutschland* was brought to a standstill south of Parchomowka by massive Soviet counterattacks. The SS recon troops made contact with the grenadiers of the *II./'T'* who had come from the east. Heavy fighting with enemy troops ensued. During the fighting the *I./SS-Pz.Rgt.3* also lost Meierdress' replacement, *SS-Ostuf.* Herbatscheck, who had been hit in the face by a shell fragment.

A *Churchill* tank passing by a German *SdKfz.232* destroyed during the fighting west of Kharkov, August 1943.

SS-Hauptsturmführer **Rudolf Säumenicht.**

SS-Ostubaf. **Otto Baum.**

Command of the armored Abteilung then passed temporarily to *SS-Ostuf.* Strobl, before being assigned permanently to *SS-Hstuf.* Rudolf Säumenicht. *SS-StuG-Abt. 'T'* was also dispatched to the Kolantejew bridgehead. All of the units there were placed under the command of *SS-Ostubaf.* Baum. *Brückenkolonne J842* was then attached to the division and along with *1.Kp./SS-Pi.-Btl. 'T'*, began to build a secondary bridge. Shortly after noon, *3.Kp./SS-Pz.Aufkl.-Abt. 'T'* finally made contact with the *Grossdeutschland*. At 2030, the *Panzerkampfgruppe* managed to reach the *'Eicke'* Regiment's bridgehead at Oleinikoff. At that time it had 15 *PzKpfw III*, 26 *PzKpfw IV* and 5 *PzKpfw VI Tiger* tanks. The *Heeresgruppe Süd* objective was now to strengthen contact between *8.Armee* and *4.Panzerarmee*. The *Totenkopf* had the mission of getting all of its units across and north of the Merla. That day was very positive for *III.Pz.Korps*: on its right flank, the *Wiking* division had achieved an important defensive success, and on its left flank the *Totenkopf* had been able to make contact with the *XXIV.Pz.Korps*. During the night of 20 August, *SS-Stubaf.* Keller noted the following results in the division's war diary: "*...The Red Army, which committed against us eight tank brigades, five rifle divisions, two motorized brigades supported by numerous anti-tank guns and two artillery regiments, lost 133 armored vehicles and 165 guns to our fire. 2,675 prisoners fell into our hands.*"

A knocked-out *Churchill* tank, August 1943.

A *Nebwelwerfer* crew loading the launcher.

The situation in the field nevertheless appeared somewhat uncertain, as can be seen in the report by *SS-Rttf.* Schiller, of the *12.Kp./'T'* : *"We were to resupply the* 12.Kp. (SS-Hstuf. *Zielke) on the other side of Kolantejew with two Kfz.70 (Horch) when night fell. When we took a small path, with lights out, towards the location still a few kilometers away, we couldn't believe our eyes: a Soviet column of combat vehicles with infantry following behind was headed straight for us. We couldn't turn back. The Soviets did not see us and continued on towards Kolantejew."*

That column, which moved at dawn on August 21, and which consisted of eight tanks, five assault guns and several trucks and jeeps, tried to break through to the northeast, rapidly crossing Kolantejew. The Germans, surprised by this unexpected thrust into their rear area, reacted quickly. Close-quarter combat ensued and lasted until 0630, with heavy losses on both sides. The SS troops suffered thirty killed, among them *SS-Stubaf.* Krauth, who was replaced at the head of the recon group by *SS-Ostuf.* Furter. *SS-Ostubaf.* Baum was wounded in the shoulder had to relinquish command of his regiment to *SS-Stubaf.* Ullrich. Meanwhile, other groups of Soviet soldiers attempted to penetrate through the German lines, taking advantage of darkness. In the morning, attacks by the Soviet First Tank Army forced *SS-Pz.Aufkl.-Abt. 'T'* to pull back between Parchomowka and Kotelewka, thus breaking its contact with *Pz.Füs.Rgt. 'GD'.* There was also fighting in the right-hand sector of *Totenkopf*; what remained of the 14th Guards Tank Brigade attempted, unsuccessfully, to cross through the lines of the *I./'TE'* at Ljubowka. Around 1400, the bridgehead at Oleinikoff was also attacked, this time from the east. Fire support by *Werfer-Rgt.52* enabled the attack to be repulsed.

SS-Sturmbannführer **Karl Ullrich.**

At 1630, *Brückenkolonne J842* was able to throw a bridge across the Merla and the *Totenkopf Panzergruppe* could be committed against Parchomowka to reestablish contact with the *Grossdeutschland*. At 1840, the panzers clashed with Soviet tanks south of Parchomowka. An hour later contact was made with *XXIV.Pz.Korps*. It was, however, a success paid for by a high price: *SS-Pz.Rgt.3* was left with twenty-four panzers and human losses had been high. Despite the state of its troops, *8.Armee* ordered that the sector assigned to the *Totenkopf* be extended as far as Parchomowka!

On August 22, the *Totenkopf* sought to consolidate it positions in the Ljubowka area. Meanwhile, its western flank continued to be weakly defended. Between the positions at Lopuchowatchyj and Schw.Pioner the only unit available was the reconnaissance group and the Soviets attacked in precisely that sector. Fourteen *T-34* tanks were thrown back in close-quarter fighting by the SS scouts. There was also fighting inside Parchomowka, where the *II./'T'* managed to hold on to the ground it had taken. Around noon, the *Totenkopf* regrouped its troops between Kotelewka and Lopuchowatchyj and struck out to the north and northeast. The attack ran up against an entire Soviet anti-aircraft regiment; many tanks, among them two Tigers, were destroyed, but the Soviet unit was completely wiped out. At 18:00 the SS troops reached the area southeast of Schw.Pioner. The attack was stopped cold at twilight due mainly to the nature of the thickly wooded terrain which impeded movement of the panzers. On the morning of 23 August, *15.(Kradsch.)Kp./'T'* succeeded in making contact with *7.Panzerdivision*, near Kotelwa. At that point, the gap that had separated *4.Panzerarmee* from *8.Armee* was by then closed. At noontime, the *Totenkopf* passed under control of *XLVII.Pz.Korps*, which assumed responsibility for the western flank of *8.Armee*, between the Merla and Worskla rivers.

Bibliography

M. Afiero, "3.SS-Panzer-Division Totenkopf, vol.II – 1943-1945", Associazione Culturale Ritterkreuz
M. Afiero, "The 3rd Waffen-SS Panzer-Division 'Totenkopf', Vol.2: 1943-1945", Schiffer Publishing Ltd

SS-Brigadeführer Otto Kumm
by Peter Mooney

A pre-war image showing Kumm in the black SS uniform.

Otto Kumm (right), seen during pre-war exercises, 1937.

Born in Hamburg at the start of October 1909, his connections to Adolf Hitler and his various organizations began at the age of 21 when he joined the *S.A.* At the start of December 1931 he moved to the fledgling *SS.* In the early 1930s he served with the *28. Standarte* and the *9. Standarte;* he was assigned the SS Number: 18 727. In August 1934 he moved to the *Hamburg Political Readiness Detachment.* By that time, he had been promoted from *SS-Sturmführer* (*Untersturmführer*) to *SS-Obersturmführer.* The mid-1930s would see Kumm being promoted further and also changing commands. By mid-September 1936, he was holding the rank of *SS-Hauptsturmführer,* three months later he moved to *SS-Regiment Deutschland,* serving as commander for various *Kompanies.* He then moved to the newly created *SS-Regiment Der Führer* in May 1938, again as a *Kompanie Commander.* He took part in the marches into Austria and the Sudetenland prior to the start of WWII. With *SS-Regiment Der Führer* he took part in the campaign in the west in 1940. During that campaign he won the Second Class Iron Cross on the 29th of May, the First Class Iron Cross on the 4th of June and the Black Wound Badge on the 8th of June. On the same day as winning his First Class Iron Cross, he moved to command of *Der Führer's, III.Battalion.* Promoted to *SS-Sturmbannführer* at the start of September 1940 and ending the year with the award of the Infantry Assault Badge in mid-December 1940. He went with *Der Führer* into Russia in the summer of 1941 and by the 11th of July, he had taken over command of the whole *Regiment.* At the start of October, he was promoted to the rank of *SS-Ostubaf.* He led his *Regiment* during the early difficult battles of *Barbarossa* in 1941, enduring many losses to his men.

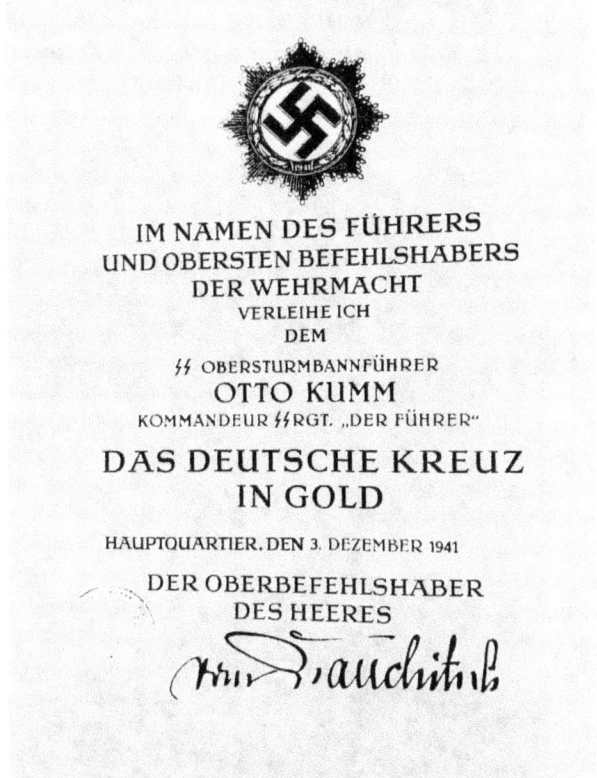

IM NAMEN DES FÜHRERS
UND OBERSTEN BEFEHLSHABERS
DER WEHRMACHT
VERLEIHE ICH
DEM
SS OBERSTURMBANNFÜHRER
OTTO KUMM
KOMMANDEUR SSRGT. „DER FÜHRER"

**DAS DEUTSCHE KREUZ
IN GOLD**

HAUPTQUARTIER. DEN 3. DEZEMBER 1941

DER OBERBEFEHLSHABER
DES HEERES

A copy of the award document for Otto Kumm's German Cross in Gold, awarded in December 1941.

An image taken straight after Kumm's award of the Knight's Cross, from the hand of Walter Model, 1942.

German Cross in Gold

By the end of 1941 he had been awarded the German Cross in Gold. That award was as a result of a Knight's Cross level recommendation, submitted by Wilhelm Bittrich, which was amended to the award of the German Cross in Gold (not unique, nor were German Cross in Gold recommendations amended to Knight's Cross approvals). The details of the submission were: "*On September 4, 1941, the reinforced Regiment 'Der Führer' attacked from Awdejewka toward the southwest. In fierce fighting, mainly involving the armored battalion, the regimental commander led in the taking of an important bridge near Rudnja at approximately 1350 hours. Shortly afterwards, the hills southwest of Rudnja were taken. Due to the immediate pursuit, which followed in the approaching darkness, the enemy unit was destroyed at Tschernotitschi where numerous weapons and equipment were captured.*

On September 15, 1941, the regiment received orders to attack from Itschnja to capture Priluki. The regiment had to attack three times against the fiercely-fighting enemy, until the edge of Kolessniki was finally captured at darkness. Through combined and reinforced reconnaissance during the night of the 16th, the enemy withdrawal could be observed at 0100 hours. With immediate pursuit at dawn, the regiment took the northern edge of Priluki. A long enemy column was destroyed and 1,400 prisoners were taken. 18 guns, four anti-tank guns, 30 mortars, numerous cars, horse-drawn vehicles and other equipment were also destroyed or captured. This success was due to SS-Obersturmbannführer Kumm's reconnaissance despite the fact that his troops were exhausted. A Russian attack by 200 troops against the regimental headquarters was repulsed by Kumm and the messengers and staff ordnance officers. The enemy suffered bloody losses.

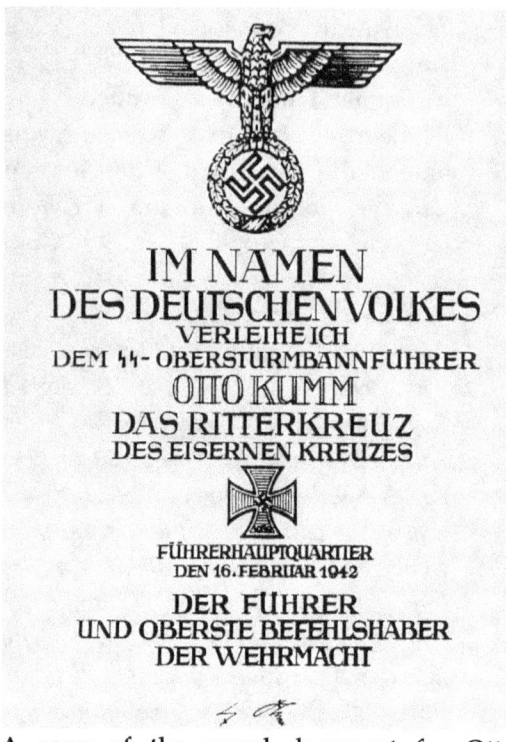
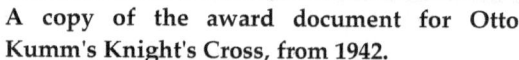

A copy of the award document for Otto Kumm's Knight's Cross, from 1942.

SS-Obersturmbannführer Otto Kumm with the Knight's Cross, 1942.

Otto Kumm, 1942.

On September 21, 1941, the regiment, reinforced by armoured units, received orders to attack against a Russian relief thrust east of Romny. With that they could surround a Russian Cavalry Division by attacking in a southward direction. Within two hours the regimental commander managed to turn his previously eastward-fighting command 90 degrees and attack in a southern direction. During fierce fighting in the village of Ssakunowo, the regiment destroyed major portions of the Russian 5th Cavalry Division. After the fighting, more than 1,000 enemy casualties were counted. Due to new march orders, the captured or destroyed equipment could not be counted. In the days between those combats, 'Der Führer' was either on the march or in combat. Due to the mud and poor Russian roads, the Regiment fought mostly on foot and during the night to continue pursuit. They took 9,466 prisoners and destroyed or captured 123 guns, 17 anti-tank guns, 40 mortars and 24 tanks. This success was possible due to the personal bravery and energy of the young regimental commander."

An image from 1942 showing Otto Kumm with his Knight's Cross and German Cross in Gold.

Soldiers of *Der Führer* in the Rshew sector.

Knights Cross to the Iron Cross

At the start of 1942, he was sent with the remnants of his regiment (about 650 men, or more akin to battalion strength) to the Rshew area. His regiment was sent to the Rshew area – despite being below strength. Here they were ordered to hold the line at all costs, as has been highlighted earlier. Otto Kumm accomplished this order, but at a very high cost. When they were relieved towards the end of February 1942, he stood with only 35 men outside the command post of Walter Model. Recognising his accomplishments, Model had already recommended Otto Kumm for the Knights Cross to the Iron Cross. The details of that recommendation contained the following information: *"Through a daring attack on January 22nd 1942 Kumm took the dominating hilly territory north of Jachino-Kelpenino. He closed the break through gap of the enemy west of Rshew, proving himself in an outstanding manner during the following heavy defensive combat with his organization and execution of the defense. During the enemy breakthrough attempts of February 7th and 8th west of Rshew, executed by strong infantry and armour forces after artillery and aerial bombing preparation, Kumm succeeded after numerous enemy penetrations, in preventing a full breakthrough. He led operations with continuous personal decisions, especially with the holding of the Regimental Command Post and occupying Ojengina with parts of* Der Führer. *During the above-mentioned defensive actions alone, two dozen tanks were destroyed under his personal leadership. He prevented, decisive for the overall situation, contact between the enemy assault force and the tenaciously holding enemy troops encircled in Kantschalowo. His personal imperturbable bearing during the heavy artillery fire and continuous tank attacks, again and again gave the troops new fighting spirit with confidence in victory."*

Waffen-SS **soldiers engaged in the Rshew sector, January 1942.**

Otto Kumm, 1942.

The above recommendation was approved on the 16th of February 1942, the day before the battle reached its' climax. The part played by Otto Kumm is well highlighted above and the significance of this regiment's actions cannot be underestimated. They held the line against everything the enemy threw at them. Walter Model personally presented the Knights Cross to Otto Kumm as he arrived at Model's Headquarters with his 35 survivors.

Immediately following this, Kumm sought permission from Model to extract his survivors from the front line so that he could reconstitute his Regiment. Model refused, due to the pressure that they still faced from the Soviets at that time, in that area. Kumm pressed his point and asked who could give him permission, to which Model directed him to seek permission from the *Reichsführer-SS*, Heinrich Himmler. He too gave Kumm a similar response, so he continued to press for who could agree to this. The only person left was Adolf Hitler himself, as Head of the Armed Forces. Otto Kumm obtained the necessary audience with Hitler and during that meeting, Kumm was astounded to learn how much Hitler knew about the actions of his Regiment and the current state of what remained. He agreed to Kumm's request, which allowed him the time to seek out survivors in the various hospitals, plus replacement troops from recruits, etc. As that was taking place, the Division of which he was part of, had been sent to France to rebuild, after the first year of action on the eastern front.

SS-Ostubaf. Otto Kumm.

Kumm inspects the new elements of the regiment *Der Führer*.

SS-Ostubaf. Otto Kumm on the Donetz Front, 1943.

During the second half of 1942, Kumm focused on ensuring *Der Führer* were ready for their next actions. During this re-fit he was awarded the Russian Front Medal, at the end of August 1942.

Knight's Cross with Oak Leaves

He returned to the eastern front in early 1943, as part of the advance elements of the newly created *SS-Panzer Korps*. Initially positioned north-east of Kharkov, the enemy pressure forced them closer to the city. He led actions around the Borki area in earky February, fighting very closely with Kameraden from the *Leibstandarte*. The fighting in that area lasted until the middle of the month, when the German advances could go

Der Führer Regiment on the Donetz Front, 1943.

no further. Otto Kumm's actions during that difficult fighting resulted in a recommendation for the Oakleaves to his existing Knight's Cross. This recommendation was written by his divisional commander, *SS-Oberführer* Herbert Vahl on the 10th of March 1943 and read as follows: "On the 11.2.43, SS-Regiment 'Der Führer' *received the order to attack the enemy whose excellent positions where in the hill and gorge filled area south of Merefa. The enemy had numerous heavy weapons, mainly anti-tank guns, in his positions. Our reconnaissance estimated his strength at seven Battalions. The* Panzer Regiment *of the* Leibstandarte *was attached to* Der Führer. *The order was: Push back the enemy along the rail line and village of Borki with tank support. After wining the first attack targets, Hills 172.3, 161.8 and 160.3, the* Panzer Regiment *would attack from a wide bow into the enemy's left flank to enable, with close cooperation, the removal of the enemy from its' strong positions. The Regiment reached its' first target and was ready in the advance positions to attack the rail line and Borki. The enemy fired heavy barrages so a further advance seemed ill advised. Here the tank attack had to force a decision. That didn't work when the enemy could not be forced from Dahgun and they were forced to withdraw. The regimental commander, observing from a most advanced position, recognized that action was an immediate must and decided to attack without tank support. This he managed with utmost cleaver use of his Battalions that ejected, pursued and destroyed the enemy. The railway was taken and the enemy lost his retreat and supply line. With that, the cut off parts of the enemy could be destroyed. Through his own decision to attack a superior strength enemy, Kumm prepared the basis for the destruction of the cut off enemy units.*

Waffen-SS Grenadiers on the Donetz front, February 1943.

On the 16.2.43, SS-Regiment 'Der Führer', received the order to reach Jefremowka and make contact with Kampfgruppe 'Meier'. *The enemy was to be encircled in a pincer movement and defeated. The* III.Battalion *of* Der Führer *attacked, but soon realized only a portion of the enemy was withdrawing towards Jefremowka with the bulk of their units moving southeast. The regimental commander decided to diverge from his original order and to attack both Jefremowka and follow the other units to destroy them as well. The result appeared a day later when the* III.Battalion *reported the destruction of an enemy Regiment. The capture of 20 guns, 30 anti-tank guns, numerous mortars, machine-guns and other equipment as well as enemy casualties was reported; Statistics that verified the original order that was diverged from and brought success from the subsequent pursuit. Additionally, during the entire attack there was a continuous struggle against snow and terrain. During the tough advance, the Regimental Commander, always to be found with the most exposed spearhead, applied his own personal energy in the quick recognition of the units' situation and in his own decisions in employing units. Consequently, the Division has to thank him that all operations were successful. The performance of both leadership and troops was extraordinary."*

Walter Kruger gives a speech to the assembled troops on the 20th of April 1943. He is about to announce the award of the Oakleaves for Otto Kumm, plus personally present Knight's Crosses to 5 of his Kameraden.

SS-Gruf. **Walter Kruger, 20th April 1943.**

This recommendation was also countersigned by Hausser who approved of the recommendation and made reference to his personal bravery. The recommendation was approved on the 6th of April 1943, giving *Das Reich* their first Oakleaves holder. The award ceremony itself, took place on the 20th of April and was well documented by war correspondents. Others who received awards (Knight's Crosses) on that same day were Christian Tychsen, Karl Worthmann, Vincenz Kaiser, Sylvester Stadler and Hans Weiss.

Walter Kruger completes the handing out of the awards, with *SS-Ostubaf.* Otto Kumm at the opposite end of that line-up. On the right, *SS-Stubaf.* Hans Weiss and *SS-Stubaf.* Kaiser.

A closer view of Otto Kumm, just after being informed that he is to receive the Oakleaves.

Knight's Cross with Oakleaves and Swords

In the aftermath of this, Kumm had to give up command of the Regiment he had led for so long and through some of its most formative combat operations. Besides the addition of the Oakleaves, he also received a promotion to *SS-Standartenführer*, on the 20th of April 1943. His next post was that of Chief of Staff for what became the *V.SS-Gebirgs Korps*. He conducted training for this role in Berlin during the late-Spring, early-Summer of 1943. Moving into the Balkans with that formation in the second half of 1943, he helped the Korp's Commander, Artur Phleps, lead the formations within it, against the operations they conducted against Tito's Partisans. His next promotion was made at the end of January 1944, when he moved to *SS-Oberführer* and at the start of February, he took over command of the *'Prinz Eugen'* Division. 1944 was a challenging year for those operating in the Balkans region and Kumm's men focused on the Nish area, remaining in that general area for the majority of 1944. The increasing enemy pressure (Soviets troops were now in this area too) and the wider strategic position for the Germans in late-1944, resulted in a general withdrawal, under enemy fire, during October. Kumm was promoted to his final rank of *SS-Brigadeführer und Generalmajor der Waffen-SS* on the 9th of November 1944.

Artur Phleps, the Commander of the *V.SS-Gebirgs-Korps* and Otto Kumm (wearing his *SS-Standartenfuhrer* rank and *gebirgsjäger* sleeve insignia), his newly appointed Chief of Staff.

SS-Obf. **Kumm, with *Prinz Eugen* officers, 1944.**

1945 would seem some notable changes for Otto Kumm. The first of those took shape in January, when *General der Flieger* Hellmuth Felmy submitted a document containing the following: "*As part of the operational withdrawal from the Balkans, 'Prinz Eugen' had withdrawn according to plan to the Nish bridgehead. This later fighting was against greatly superior forces in the area of Leskovac-Bela-Palanka (six Bulgarian infantry divisions and one tank brigade) and Zajecar (three Russian divisions). The swift evacuation of the 700 wounded, supplies and installations, such as the command headquarters and anti-aircraft guns was required.* **Brigadeführer** *Kumm's proposed route northwards through Aleksinac was already blocked north of there by strong Russian forces and could not be opened up by the 12.10.1944, with a weak one battalion force at Kumm's disposal. Communication with the Korps was severed so the divisional commander decided to send this motorized column west through Mramor-Prokuplje.*

SS-Standartenführer Otto Kumm seen in the performance of his Chief of Staff duties for the *V.SS-Gebirgs Korps.*

Otto Kumm, showing his *SS-Standartenführer* rank and Knight's Cross with Oakleaves.

Kumm receive from the hands of Hitler the *Oakleaves.*

The Nish bridgehead had to be held right up to the 14.10 against the enemy exerting strong pressure. The Morava bridge, destroyed near Mramor, was repaired on the morning of 13.10. and the column of some 1,000 vehicles did not fully cross until 0900 hours the next day due to bad weather. Following the motorized elements, the horse-drawn transport moved out. At 1045 hours a Bulgarian division reinforced by a tank brigade attacked the withdrawal route from the south, concentrating on the left flank around Merosina where the divisional headquarters was located. Three Luftwaffe *Kompanies that had been sent to protect the southern flank were routed. SS-Brigadeführer Kumm immediately gathered all available men (about 40 with three light machine guns) and with them held the southern outskirts of Merosina. Portions of the II./Geb.Jg.Rgt.13 were ordered to execute a diversionary attack from the southern outskirts of Nish, but were unable to as the battalion was itself under attack by enemy tanks and infantry.*

A formal portrait of Otto Kumm, showing his *SS-Standartenführer* rank, Knight's Cross with Oakleaves (this was one of the signed images sent to me by Otto Kumm).

An image from 1944 showing Otto Kumm in the Balkans, the *Gebirgsjäger* insignia can be seen on his cap.

The column of vehicles was shot to pieces by tanks, artillery and anti-tank guns. Drivers and horse-drawn vehicles were routed.

The courageous resistance of the divisional commander held up the enemy long enough for the vehicles with wounded and other parts of the column to move west and later to Pristina. By 1300 hours the enemy had blocked both sides of Merosina and had penetrated the town with infantry. Kumm then withdrew and, after expending all ammunition, fought his way through to the headquarters of the II./SS-Gebirgsjäger Regiment 13. From there he commanded the retreat of the battalion from the Nish bridgehead and the regrouping of reachable other units from the Division at Dudulajce. The withdrawal and regrouping was accomplished, but all artillery was abandoned.

Due to the lack of ammunition and heavy weapons, the divisional commander decided to avoid big battles and fight his way over the ridge of the Jastrebac mountains, through partisan bands, in order to make contact with our troops in the Ibar Valley. After an extremely hard march with 4,000 men and 1,000 horses without sufficient food, they reached the valley and camped in the Usce-Bare area. Through this daring operation, SS-Brigadeführer Kumm evaded being surrounded by a vastly superior enemy and retained troops with fighting capability."

He was approved for the addition of the Swords to his existing Knight's Cross with Oakleaves, on the 17th of March 1945. Back in early February, Kumm had moved to become the fourth and final commander of the *1. SS-Panzer Division 'Leibstandarte SS-Adolf Hitler'.* They were in Hungary by then and engaging a significant Soviet offensive, aimed at Budapest and moving to the west from there. Whilst the honour of being in command of this formation would have existed, in Kumm's own words, he recalls that the division he handed was not the elite and strong division it had once been in its heyday. It was a burnt out shell and at the stage of fighting for its existence, against a very strong enemy. It was their former commander, Joseph 'Sepp' Dietrich, that made the actual award of Kumm's Swords.

An image of Kumm from late-1944, with his newly acquired SS-*Brigadeführer* rank being worn on his collars. From the Left, *SS-Ostuf.* Mayer, *SS-Staf.* Deutsch, *SS-Hstuf.* Niedermeier, *SS-Stubaf.* Neumann, *SS-Brigdf.* Kumm e *SS-Ostuf.* Kirchner.

Waffen-SS Soldiers on the Hungarian Front, 1945.

A chance to get these from the hand of Hitler was not an option at that stage of the war. Kumm led his men westwards, almost being encircled by the Soviets and having to see his division fighting in a piecemeal and split up manner, which reduced their effectiveness. The fighting continued to move westwards into Austria, with the *Leibstandarte* operating to the south of Vienna and in a general westerly route towards the Enns River. It was there that he surrendered his division to American forces, on the 8th of May, although some of his troops continued to drift through until the cut off deadline. Like the majority of his *Waffen-SS* Kameraden, he was placed in a prisoner of

A formal image to show Otto Kumm's final rank of *SS-Brigadeführer*, plus the Swords to the Knight's Cross with Oakleaves. This signed version was another photo sent to me by Otto Kumm.

A German *Jagdpanzer.IV* on the Austrian Front.

war camp where they waited to see what the post-conflict world looked like for them. Any illusions they may have had were soon clarified / dispelled, when the military organisation he had been a part of for more than 13-years was classed as an illegal organisation by the Allied powers. That placed extreme pressure on them all to be able to forge an existence as they began to be released from the prisoner or war camps. Their homeland turned their backs on them and many of them struggled to find employment; many that did, found that the nature of the work offered, was amongst the dirtiest and unpleasant available. It was realities like that, which prompted Otto Kumm to form what became known as HIAG. (*Hilfsgemeinschaft auf Gegenseitigkeit der Angehörigen der ehemaligen Waffen-SS*, or Mutual Aid Association of former Waffen-SS members). That was in 1950 and as the association took shape and word spread, many former *Waffen-SS* soldiers were able to see an improvement in their post-war lives. Re-unions began too and they carried on into the mid-2000s.

It was at one such re-union, that of the *I.Panzer Korps*, that I met Otto Kumm for the first time. It was evident that he was held in high esteem. Despite me being unknown to him, he took the time to sign some items I had with me then. That was in 1999 and the following year, my interaction with him increased, by accident! There was always an official function held on the last night of the re-union. At the end of the evening when I was walking back to the car, I noticed Otto

Kumm and his wife in the middle of the car park, but with no-one accompanying them. I approached them to check on whether they were being collected.

Myself and Otto Kumm at the *I.Panzer Korps* reunion.   *SS-Ostubaf.* **Otto Kumm, 1943.**

To my surprise, his response was 'no'. I rectified that immediately and together with 2 friends, the 5 of us returned to the hotel. During the journey Otto Kumm spoke to me in English, enquiring about, '*driving on the wrong side of the road*' and, '*driving an English car on German roads, with the steering wheel being in the wrong place*'. This was amusing, but I was still astounded that someone who was in the position he was (official Head of that Korps reunions organisation) had been left to his own devices. I wrote to him afterwards and he referenced the journey along with sending some signed images. (for those of you who receive this magazine regularly, the evening in question was the same one that resulted in me driving Otto Gunsche, Hubert Meyer and Johannes Goehler to the same function on the way out – see previous editions).

Whilst I continued to attend the re-union when I could, Otto Kumm's attendance stopped, as his health declined. He passed away on the 23rd of March 2004. His military career is without doubt one of the most impressive I have come across. His consistent abilities were recognised at the highest of levels, in the form of awards and promotions. Always finding himself in the hottest of hot-spots, he always had the lives of his men in the forefront on his mind, saving many thousands of their lives through his actions in battle. That mind-set carried on post-war with the HIAG organisation. His legacy is evidenced and it is understandable why his Kameraden held him in the high esteem they did. I am grateful for the chance to have met him and for his help in some of my book / history projects. I hope that you have found this article of interest.

The Barbarigo on the Anzio front
by Massimiliano Afiero - 4th part

A destroyed *Sherman* on the Anzio Front, May 1944.

Marines of the *Barbarigo* on the Anzio Front, May 1944.

German patrol engaged in combat, near a 20mm *Flak* gun.

On May 1, 1944, the *First Special Force* units attacked the southern sector defended by the *Barbarigo*, a cultivated area called by the Allies the 'plantation area'. A battalion of the 2nd Regiment of the *First Special Force* moved towards Borgo Sabotino, supported by a company of light tanks, a platoon of self-propelled guns, the assault guns of the 81st Reconnaissance Battalion and an armored car section. As soon as the attack began, the outpost of Cerreto Alto was evacuated and its defenders fell back on the main line to avoid ending up being surrounded. Not being able to avoid the minefields, numerous Allied soldiers ended up as victims of the explosive devices. Also along the beach, the American tanks ended up on the mines: at least two light tanks were destroyed. Immediately afterwards the Italian-German artillery entered into action, which began to strike the attacking forces, forcing them to fall back under the protection of a smokescreen. With this latest attack having been repulsed, a few days of calm followed. The battalion's command took the opportunity to carry out some changes on the front line: on 4 May, the 4th Company replaced the 2nd, taking up a position between the Strada Nascosa-Strada della Persicara junction and the Gorgolicinio foundry. During that same night, a 4th Company patrol made a probe, with the mission to infiltrate the American lines and carry out a reconnaissance in the rear.

May 1944: one of the last shellings by Allied artillery on the city of Littoria.

A *Barbarigo* officer on the Anzio front, May 1944.

Among the marines who took part in the action was Gavino Casella, eighteen years old, originally from Rome. Casella was discovered by enemy sentries and ended up under enemy fire: he still managed to complete his mission and to return unharmed carrying the requested information. On May 5, *Oberst* von Schellerer, commander of a combat group of the *715.Inf.Division*, awarded the Iron Cross Second Class to Midshipman Mario Riondino. On that same day, the 2nd Company was transferred to the Malconsiglio road, near Lake Fogliano, where it resumed training. On 8 May, following an order from German headquarters, the 2nd Company was transferred to Cisterna, to be engaged in fortification work; its camp was in an olive grove, five kilometers from the work area. Initially the transfer of the marines to the operational area took place on German trucks, then in the following days, it took place on foot and always under the incessant fire of enemy artillery.

A *Sherman* tank in the Cisterna sector, May 1944.

A German mortar on the Anzio Front, May 1944.

American tanks and soldiers in the Cisterna sector.

The marines of the *Barbarigo* were engaged in the construction of defensive works and in the laying of minefields.

New clashes

By 7 May, Barbarigo's losses had been 29 killed, 71 wounded and 19 missing. There were also 27 cases of desertion reported. During the night of 11 May, an Italian patrol consisting of marines of the 3rd Company, was engaged in a deep incursion between the enemy lines, successfully reporting information on the location of the strongholds and on the movements of the American units. The next day, the 1st Company, still stationed along the coast, suffered a massive naval bombardment by a cruiser and two enemy destroyers. Fortunately there were no losses.

On 9 May, the 1st Company left the Terracina sector to relieve the 3rd Company on the front line. The marines of the 3rd Company arrived in Terracina on German vehicles: here, they were placed in the operational command of an officer of the *15.Panzergrenadier-Division*, *Leutnant* Pabst. The marines took up positions in a series of bunkers, sheltered from continuous naval bombardments.

On 11 May 1944, the Allies launched Operation *Diadem*, with the aim of breaking the German defenses on the *Gustav* Line and opening the Liri Valley, the main road to Rome. This forced the Germans to fall back on the *Hitler* line.

On May 15th, Marshal Rodolfo Graziani inspected the 3rd Company and on the occasion also gave a small talk to the marines, from which we extract this significant phrase: "... *From the point of view of the honor and dignity of our country, your Company alone is worth an entire Army Corps* ".

Meanwhile, the fighting continued for 1st and 4th companies, especially by patrols in no-man's land. Enemy artillery fire continued to claim victims.

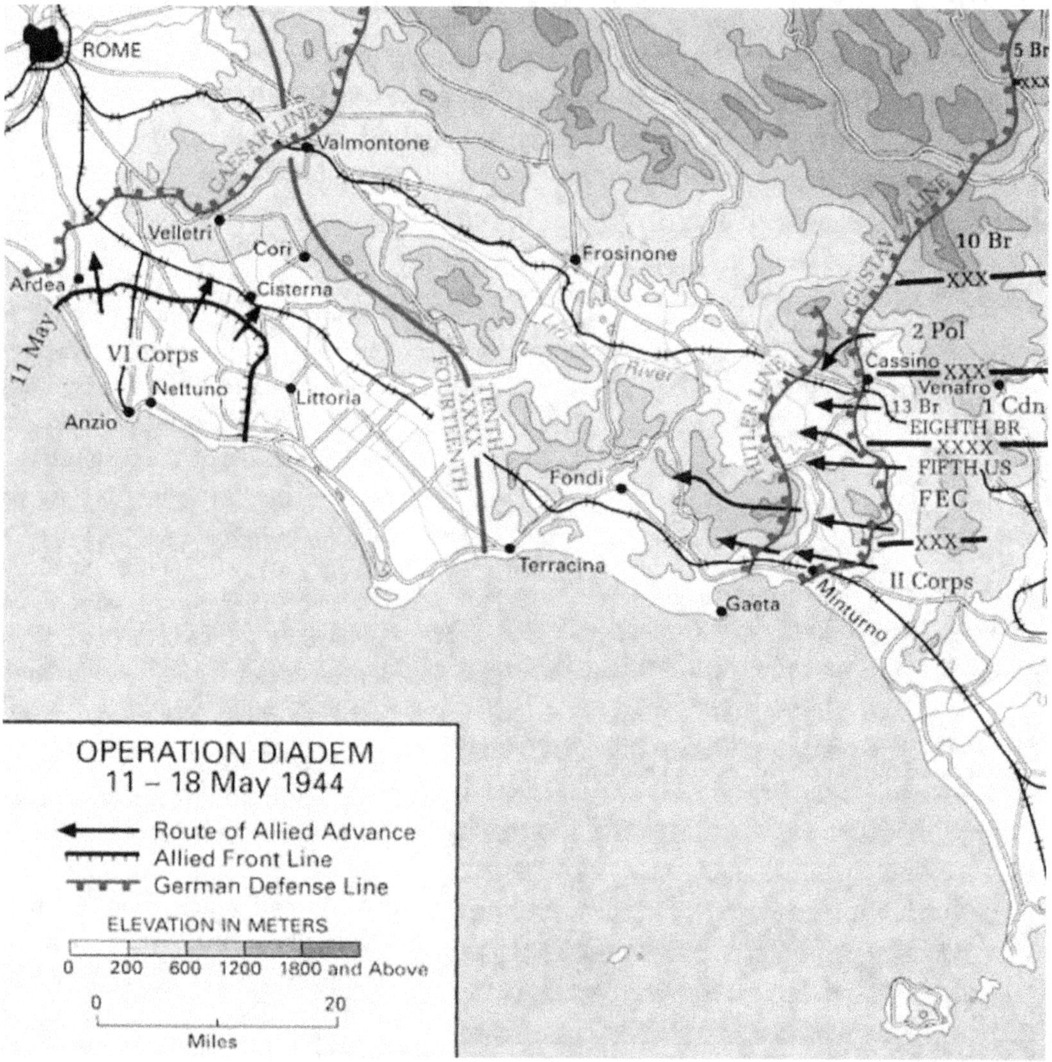

OPERATION DIADEM
11 – 18 May 1944

← Route of Allied Advance
↤↤↤ Allied Front Line
↤↤↤ German Defense Line

ELEVATION IN METERS

0   200   600   1200   1800 and Above

0   20
Miles

German soldiers captured at Cisterna, 1944.

On May 23, 1944, an official German communiqué reported that a few days earlier, Field Marshal Kesserling, supreme commander of the German Armed Forces in Italy, had sent a telegram to the commander of the Xᵃ Flottiglia Mas, Junio Valerio Borghese, to praise the Barbarigo's magnificent behavior, defining the Italian volunteers:

'... *as the best soldiers of the Nettuno front for discipline and courage*'.

A destroyed American *M-10*, May 1944.

A Funker belonging to a *Flakbatterie* receiving fire cordinates, Italy, Nettuno Front.

Withdrawal order

On May 23, the Allied forces also attacked the *Hitler* Line and on that same day, the 6th US Corps attacked the German troops in Anzio, launching Operation *Buffalo*: this involved the conquest of Cisterna, the breakthrough of the German line and the advance between the Alban Hills and the Lepini Hills. At that moment, Barbarigo's forces were dispersed along the entire southern side of the bridgehead, subordinate to different tactical commands and without any connection between them. The attack made by the American 1st Armored Division and the *First Special Force*, aimed at the conquest of Valmontone, to cut off the retreat of the Italian-German troops withdrawing from the *Gustav* Line and from the eastern side of the bridgehead. Particularly exposed were the positions of the 3rd Company in Terracina, isolated from the rest of the battalion. The Allied forces, after passing through the *Gustav* Line, attacked the city from the south. On May 23, the company received the order from Leutnant Pabst to fall back. The movement took place under the bombing of Allied aviation. Lieutenant Enzo Leoncini divided his men into teams of ten men, making them move at a intervals, to limit losses as much as possible. Ordering the movements with his whistle, Leoncini was the last to move. The march lasted about seven hours, until sunset. When the marines finally arrived near a power plant, they discovered that they had not suffered any losses, which was a real miracle. The next day, the whole company arrived in Sermoneta, after traveling on foot, twelve kilometers. About twenty marines were immediately deployed to the outposts, along the stretch held by the 4th Company, which had been abandoned two hours earlier by the Germans. The rest of the company, divided into groups, was deployed at Tor Monticchio and Tor Tre Ponti, subordinate to *Kampfgruppe von Schellerer*.

Lieutenant Giulio Cencetti.

A *Sherman* tank destroyed on the Anzio Front, May 1944.

Let's listen to the testimony of Lieutenant Giulio Cencetti[1]: "... *Separated from the battalion, in Terracina, the 3rd Company sees the Germans retreat. The field radio is the last to leave. Now Lieutenant Leoncini is alone with his men. Facing the mountains, the only side from which up until then it was not necessary to bother to worry about guarding, we can now hear explosions and furious fighting getting closer and closer. The Allied Fifth Army, having broken through the front at Cassino, seeks to exploit its success and moves forward. But Leoncini has no orders. He only knows that he must stay. The 'Barbarigo' headquarters had always been close to his troops, but this time it has been two days that he has had no news from them. It is useless to monitor 'The sea front' since it is from the landward side that the offensive will take place, and from Terracina to Sermoneta, there are many kilometers! The dams that have been blown up flood the state highway that is the only way to link up with the battalion, and it is heavily hit by aircraft and by enemy artillery. The boys look at the lieutenant who, with his typical reserve as a gentleman from Brescia, still manages to smile at everyone: he believes in the duty he has to do, he puts his faith in the headquarters and those great anti-tank ditches dug by the Germans on the main road, from the foot of the mountain to the sea, he thinks they can give him the security of not being surrounded immediately. But, on the evening of the third day, the first shots fall upon the company and Leoncini sees the anti-tank ditches being filled by the enemy, one by one ... He decides to move towards Sermoneta. It is a forced march, exhausting along miles of road being hit by shellfire. In the middle of the night, halfway along the way, a motorbike comes to meet them: it is Captain Marchesi who, alone in that hell, ventured towards the company to bring news, because he did not want it to be cut off: he was the voice of the headquarters stating that it would never neglect even a single marine".*

US infantrymen and tanks pass knocked-out German tanks on the Anzio Front, May 1944.

The area south of Rome, where the Marò of the *Barbarigo* were engaged in May 1944.

A German *Panther* on the Anzio Front, May 1944.

The *Barbarigo* had not received precise dispositions on how to face the new enemy offensive and effect a possible withdrawal. It was not until late morning of May 24, Lieutenant Vallauri, after going to the command of the *Kampfgruppe von Schellerer*, was informed that the withdrawal of all the Italian-German forces was to begin at 9.00 pm that same evening. In the afternoon, the time was moved up to 18:00, but it was not possible to transmit the new order to all the units, which thus withdrew independently, with no more contact with the headquarters. Vallauri, with the Tross[2], elements of the headquarters company and the infirmary, received the order to fall back at 2.30 pm on 24 May, following the German columns and reaching Sezze Romano. Here, he received the order from the battalion command to retreat to Rome.

The fate of the 1st Company

Also on 24 May, the 1st Company was ordered by the commander of the *Barbarigo* to detach two platoons, the 1st and the 2nd, under the orders of Lieutenant Mario Betti, to the 5th company of the 676th German Grenadier Regiment and another platoon to the 6th company of the 735th German Grenadier Regiment, retreating to new positions between Sermoneta and Sezze and between Sezze and Privello. The group led by Betti, began to fall back with the German grenadiers around 17:30: along the way, some vehicles came to recover the

German soldiers, leaving the Italians to continue on foot. When the Betti group arrived in Sermoneta, the Germans had already left the position. Left without orders, Betti then decided to continue towards Sezze Romano, where he arrived at dawn the next day. There, he met only a German engineer unit, engaged in destroying bridges. The commander of the German unit informed him that the headquarters of *Kampfgruppe von Schellerer* had probably moved to Cori. The march continued towards the latter location.

Italian and German soldiers captured in Cisterna, May 1944.

German *Fallschirmjäger.*

Midshipman Alessandro Tognoloni.

On the afternoon of May 25, Betti's group, reinforced in the meantime by fifty German stragglers, arrived in Cori: however, there was no trace of the German headquarters. But at that very moment, the American forward elements arrived and the firefight with the marines began. Once the enemy threat had been distanced, Betti decided to continue towards Segni, where he arrived at 1.30 pm on May 26th: there, after having recovered two civilian trucks, he loaded his remaining men and went with them to Rome. The rest of the company continued to fight, later to return to Rome and rejoin the battalion.

The fate of the 2nd Company

On May 23rd, the 2nd Company was transferred by truck to the Sermoneta area. Here, Lieutenant Paolo Posio, commander of the company, ordered Midshipman. Alessandro Tognoloni, with a group of forty men, formed by the reinforced 3rd Platoon, near the Via Appia in Cisterna, to establish a stronghold and block the advance of the Americans. The marines were equipped only with light weapons including machine guns, rifles, and some *Panzerfausts*. On board another truck column, the combat group reached its assigned position. Tognoloni arranged his men about a kilometer west of the state road, clogged by retreating troops. As soon as the first units of the American 3rd Division were sighted, supported by tanks, the battle began. We read the testimony of Tognoloni himself[3]: "... *I made contact with my platoon with other small forces present on the site and after a short rest each team expanded to a defensive line. Of course, the war was all around us, but the 'music' as Posio calls it intended to stop those on the Appia, and then shortened its range to fire on us as soon as we were identified. It was only a moment before the May grain parted and four or five Shermans engaged the nearest target. At 7:30 AM fire from all of the tanks hit us and many marines and I were hit, however our reaction led the enemy to believe that he had a far more substantial presence to overcome, so much so that the tanks stopped. We found refuge behind a farmhouse in which in covered trenches had been prepared and which were subjected to furious mortar fire all day, as well as during the night. Meanwhile, I was wounded and exhausted and was receiving news of the other active and heroic squads until were wiped out. At midnight I ordered the few survivors to withdraw; I and a few others, hampered by wounds, remained soldiers without strength, but were considered by the enemy to be a fierce outpost. Fire continued to fall upon us for the rest of the following day (May 24th) until we were captured at 17 PM. And along a path marked by strips of white cloth to avoid the minefields, I was carried on a stretcher by German prisoners, I was carried to the rear area and then to the hospital of Anzio. I can conclude that the enemy's caution and our presence that determined it prevented the enemy from reaching the Appia for 36 hours. Our losses were serious. Most of those who died are still in Rome in the Verano cemetery* ".

Aerial photo of Anzio and Nettuno, in the background the Lepini mountains (*U.S. Army*).

German soldiers during the retreat to Rome, May 1944.

A German *StuG.III* and a destroyed *Sherman*, May 1944.

As the enemy tanks were approaching his position, Tognoloni, while wounded, managed to rise and push himself forward, with a pistol in one hand and a hand grenade in the other.

US infantrymen pass knocked-out *Sherman* tank.

German soldiers captured by US infantrymen, May 1944.

US infantrymen under enemy fire, May 1944.

He ended up being cut down by the fire of a heavy machine gun from a *Sherman*. He was given up for dead by the marines who returned to the unit[4]. He was posthumously awarded the Gold Medal for Military Valor.

Sergeant Edoardo Calcinotti, 31 years old from La Spezia, also distinguished himself in these clashes. With his team he was busy defending his position from enemy armored attacks, until he was left with only three men. Three tanks approached, Calcinotti succeeded in disabling one with a magnetic mine, but while he tried to attack the other tanks, he was killed by enemy fire. He was awarded the Silver Medal for Military Valor posthumously.

The company continued to be engaged in defensive fighting to try to slow down the Allied advance at the foot of the Lepini Mountains and cover the retreat of German forces from the Cassino front. In two days of fierce fighting, the Americans lost more than a hundred tanks just to be able to penetrate the defensive line in the Cisterna sector. The two last platoons of the company finally received the order to fall back on Cori, along with elements of the 3rd Company, and to establish the connection with the reserve company of the 735th German Grenadier Regiment. On the afternoon of May 24, the marines began their march on foot to Rome. In the night between 24 and 25 May, near the station of Torretta Corana, a violent bombardment by Allied aviation claimed numerous victims, thirty-two killed and seriously wounded. The survivors continued in the direction of Sermoneta and Cori. Without further marching orders, Midshipman. Posio decided to continue towards Giulianello. Around 12:00, the 'marò' ran into a motorized column of the 1st Italian SS company, boarding its trucks. Shortly afterwards, the same column was attacked by Allied aircraft and was completely destroyed. The few survivors, still led by Posio, arrived on the 27th in Artena and from there continued on to Rome.

American infantry units entering in Littoria, May 1944.

German soldiers on the Anzio front, May 1944.

The fate of the 3rd Company

As already seen previously, on 24 May, the company found itself divided into three groups, two located on the outposts in front of the IV company and in the area of Littoria and one aggregated to the II company. The group present in Littoria, comprising fifty marines, at 3:00 pm that same day, received the order to settle in the west of Norma, on a defensive line about three kilometers long and establish the connection with the 1st battalion of the 735th German Grenadier Regiment. At dawn on 25 May, the g.m. Leoncini with his marines, stood on the new positions and established the connection with the German departments. At 2:00 pm, the two German companies on the flanks withdrew. Soon after, the first American avant-gardes attacked the positions of the marines. Sergeant Natale Milella, who commanded a machine-gun team, distinguished himself in these fights. After exhausting all the ammunition, Milella ordered her men to retreat, remaining alone to cover the maneuver. He managed to resist for a long time and only when his position was overtaken by enemy forces, he broke loose and managed to rejoin the company. Leoncini's group, after resisting enemy attacks for hours, fell back fighting on the mountain on which Norma stands, joining other German units. From here, the marines came first to Artena, then to Valmontone and finally continued towards Rome.

The fate of the 4th Company

The order to retreat having reached it with delay, the bulk of the 4th Company received the order to fall back to Norma on the evening of May 24 and to join the 2nd Battalion of the 735th Grenadier Regiment. To cover the maneuver, a small *Kampfgruppe* was formed, comprising two non-commissioned officers and 20 marines, placed under the orders of a German non-commissioned officer. During the clashes with the Allied forces, this rearguard force was completely destroyed. Between May 25 and 26, the rest of the company, reinforced by a platoon from the 1st Company, continued to fight alongside the German grenadiers. On May 27, at the behest of Major Winter, commander of I./735, the company retreated to Montelanico, where the marines were integrated into a fighting group led by Oberst Hepp, comprising around 80 German stragglers and 60 marines from the company . On May 28, at the behest of German headquarters, Oberst Hepp ordered the marines to hand over their weapons (not without some opposition), who then continued their retreat, alone and unarmed, to the capital.

The fate of the gunners

The survivors of the 5th Cannon Company, on the evening of May 24th, received the order to fall back on Tor Tre Ponti and establish contact with the German artillerymen. The company then continued on Cori, where it met up with Lieutenant Junior Grade Carnevale, commander of the San Giorgio Group, who ordered the marines to fall back on Giulianello. Having lost its last surviving gun during an Allied bombing lost, the remnants of the company made it back to Rome.

The San Giorgio Group's batteries, for their part, continued to fire throughout May 24 to cover the retreat of the other units. Since there were no vehicles left to tow the guns, when the order to retreat arrived, all the guns were destroyed. On foot, the artillerymen continued in the direction of Giulianello and then of San Cesareo, where the order to return to Rome arrived from the battalion headquarters.

Notes

[1] From "*Gli ultimi in grigioverde*", p. 1095.

[2] The logistics train of the unit.

[3] From "*Duri a morire - storia del Battaglione Barbarigo*", page 61.

[4] Recovered by American medical personnel, after intense medical treatment, he ended the war in a prison camp in Texas.

Bibliography

Mario Bordogna, "*Junio Valerio Borghese e la X^a Flottiglia MAS*", Mursia, Milano, 2007
Guido Bonvicini, "*Decima Marinai! Decima Comandante!*", Mursia, Milano
Daniele Lembo, "*I fantasmi di Nettunia*", Edizioni Settimo Sigillo
Marino Perissinotto, "*Duri a morire - storia del Battaglione Barbarigo*", Ermanno Albertelli Editore
Perissinotto, Panzarasa, "*Come la Fenice*", Editoriale Lupo
Giorgio Pisanò, "*Gli ultimi in grigioverde*", C.D.L. Edizioni

THE PRICE OF THE OATH
The last battle of the Charlemagne Division
by Tomasz Borowski

SS-Brigadeführer **Krukenberg.**

General **Helmuth Weidling.**

....Between midnight and 3:00 am on April 25,[1] Krukenberg, accompanied by his aide, *SS-Hauptsturmführer* Pachur, jumped into a commandeered car. *SS-Untersturmführer* Patzak took the wheel and they headed for the Reich Chancellery. The whole trip took them only half an hour. They did not have to make any stops as Berlin seemed devoid of all human life. There was an ominous silence enveloping the city, only sparsely interrupted by distant blasts from Russian artillery. Moreover, the city appeared completely lacking any defensive entrenchments, even though, in February 1945, Hitler had declared the whole city to be a fortress. Where were any of the troops? Where were the cannons? The barricades? And where was this so-called fortress? Having parked their car in front of the Chancellery's bunker, guarded by sentries, Krukenberg and Pachur went inside. The *SS-Brigadeführer* informed the sentries that he wanted to meet General Krebs. They told him Krebs was busy and asked him to take a seat in the waiting room. Minutes went by at a crawling pace, then turned into hours. In the close and hot atmosphere of the room they had to wait in, they reflected upon how obviously ill-prepared Berlin was to push back any assault by the Russians. The situation was so bad that perhaps the Soviets would not need much more than a surprise attack by a well-trained commando to enter and kill or capture the *Führer* himself. Finally, around 3:30 a.m. three hours later Krukenberg was allowed to see Krebs, who was accompanied by General Wilhelm Burgdorf[2]. Both generals were surprised seeing Krukenberg. Krebs mentioned that 48 hours previously, he had ordered many officers and their men around Berlin to get to the capital post-haste,

but only Krukenberg had arrived so far. He then proceeded to brief Krukenberg on the situation. There wasn't much new, only that there was a chance to save the city, that the

Soviets were weakening, that Wenck's army was close and bringing reinforcements, and that future help from the Western Allies against the Bolsheviks was very possible[3]. Next, Krebs ordered Krukenberg to report in the morning to General Helmuth Weidling, who was put in command of the Berlin Area Defence the previous day, on 24 April[4].

Berlin, April 1945. German soldiers engaged in removing rubble from the streets.

Volkssturm **members in Berlin, April 1945.**

His command post was located on Fehrberlliner Platz near the Hohenzollerndamm. Before leaving, Krukenberg also asked where he could find *SS-Obergruppenführer* Hermann Fegelein, a *Waffen-SS* liaison officer to Adolf Hitler's HQ, to whom he was obliged to report. With Fegelein nowhere to be found, Krukenberg was asked to come back to the Chancellery in a few days. Nobody knew what was about to happen. Shortly after 4:00 a.m., Krukenberg and Pachur left the bunker. The roads were still empty. Before 5:00 a.m., they were back in the *Reichssportfeld*. The sun was dawning and the sky was clear. The Frenchmen still slept. Most of them enjoyed uninterrupted, heavy sleep, despite the sounds of Russian artillery echoing closer and closer. Krukenberg was greeted by Henri Fenet, who was impatiently awaiting orders. He told him he was to see General Weidling, and as soon as he knew which sector they were to take, he would send *SS-Untersturmführer* Patzak to carry the news. Fenet could only wait[5]. When Krukenberg and Pachur went to get some rest, the men of the French SS-Assault Battalion rose, one by one, woken by their NCOs. They were called to assembly and everyone made their own preparations for the upcoming battle. The men washed themselves in the waters of the Havel, shaved, cleaned their uniforms and greased their guns. To occupy their time and thoughts, they sang. *Waffen-Hauptsturmführer* Fenet rearranged the whole battalion[6], but it only amounted to giving new numbers to the companies who arrived in Berlin. The final result was as follows:

Waffen-Hstuf. **Henri Fenet.**

Waffen-Ostuf. **Pierre Michel.**

Franzosische SS-Sturmbataillon[7]
CO: *Waffen-Hauptsturmführer* Henri Fenet
EXO: *SS-Ostuf.* Hans-Joachim von Wallenrodt

1. Duty Officer: *Waffen-Ustuf.* Jacques Frantz
2. Duty Officer: *Waffen-St.Oberjunker* Alfred Douroux

1. Kompanie
CO: *Waffen-Untersturmführer* Jean Labourdette
EXO: *Waffen-Standartenoberjunker* Jean Cossard
Waffen-Standartenoberjunker Jean-Marie Croisile
1. platoon: *Waffen-St.Oberjunker* Andre Boulmier
2. platoon: *Waffen-St.Oberjunker* Maxime De Lacaze
3. platoon: *W-St.Obj.* Jacques Le Maignan De Kerangat

2. Kompanie
CO: *Waffen-Obersturmführer* Pierre Michel
1. platoon: *Waffen-Standartenjunker* Marcel Hardy
2. platoon: *Waffen-St.Obj.* Jean-Philippe Neron
3. platoon: *Waffen-Oberscharführer* Marc Montgour

3. Kompanie
CO: *Waffen-Hauptscharführer* Pierre Rostaing
EXO: *Waffen-Standartenoberjunker* Jean Dumoulin
1. platoon: *Waffen-Standartenoberjunker* Raoul Ginot
2. platoon: *Waffen-St.Obj.* Gaston Baumgartner
3. platoon: its members were in one of the trucks that broke down on their way to Berlin

4. Kompanie
CO: *Waffen-Oberscharführer* Jean Ollivier
EXO: *Waffen-Standartenjunker* Serge Protopopoff
1. platoon: *Waffen-Unterscharführer* Fieselbrand
2. platoon: *Waffen-Standartenjunker* Sellier
3. platoon: *Waffen-Unterscharführer* Paul Sauvageot

Honour Guard (*Kampfschule*)
CO: *SS-Obersturmführer* Wilhelm Weber
1. platoon: *Waffen-Oberscharführer* Pierre Bousquet
2. platoon: *Waffen-Uscha.* Jean Aime-Blanc
3. platoon: *Waffen-Uscha.* Gérard Fontenay

Member of the Hitler Youth with a *Panzerfaust* in the defense of Berlin, April 1945.

Volkssturm defending *Anhalt Station* in Berlin.

SS-Brigdf. Ziegler (right) on the Narwa Front, 1944.

After a few hours' rest, Krukenberg went to Hohenzollerndamm to report to General Weidling's command post, accompanied – again – by Pachur and Patzak. This time around they did encounter a few patrols and barricades on the streets, yet still no sign of a proper military presence capable of defensive action. Upon arrival, they were first taken to *Oberst* Dufving, *LVI Panzer Corps* Chief of Staff, and then introduced to Weidling. He told Krukenberg that he had arrived in Berlin two days before and agreed to take command of the city's defences, even though he did not agree with how his superiors envisioned that defence. Weidling had a very small force at his disposal: remnants of the *LVI Panzer Corps*, which were still busy licking their wounds from their bloody battles, poorly trained and equipped troops of the *Volkssturm*, *Luftwaffe* auxiliary units and some youths from the *Hitlerjugend*. Beyond their high morale and incredible fighting spirit, their military value was negligible[8]. In the presence of his Chief-of-Staff, Weidling told Krukenberg that the southeast sector of the city one of 10 marked as Defence Sector C (*Verteidigungsabschnit C*), was assigned to *11.SS-Freiwilligen Panzer Grenadier Division 'Nordland'* under *SS-Brigadeführer* Joachim Ziegler's command. Ziegler was later charged with insubordination, loss of control and inability to command his unit, and he was removed from his post and Krukenberg put in his place. Having received the order and passing command over to

Krukenberg, Ziegler was to report to the Reich Chancellery post-haste. It is worth elaborating on *SS-Brigadeführer* Ziegler's dismissal as it is still a subject of discussion among many historians of the late stages of the war on the Eastern Front. Wilhelm Tieke believes Ziegler's discharge to be the result of his inability to keep up the defence around the Spree-Teltow Channel. Furthermore, Tieke admits that the decision to dismiss Ziegler was nonsensical as it was not possible for the decimated '*Nordland*' Division to keep its positions any longer[9]. Antony Beevor, on the other hand, claims that Ziegler saw the futility of the fight and didn't want his soldiers to die in vain. Just before his removal from the post, Ziegler even allowed *SS-Hstuf.* Pehrsson to visit the Swedish embassy and see if the Swedes from their unit could count on any support in case of their return home.

Hans-Gosta Pehrsson.

SS-Obf. Ziegler and *SS-Ogruf.* Steiner on the Baltic Front, 1944.

Soldiers and Civilians under the bombing.

General Weidling's Chief-of-Staff, Colonel Refior, believed that Ziegler had received secret orders from Himmler to retreat to Schlezwig-Holstein[10]. *SS-Obergruppenführer* Felix Steiner, Ziegler's direct superior and commander of the Steiner Army Group, also came to his defence: "SS-Brigadeführer *Ziegler did all in his power to avoid the impending doom. The command, however, reacted with suspicion to his request to move the division[11] to the outer ring of Berlin's defences This would make it impossible to attempt to cross to the West, a plan Ziegler had to abandon*"[12]. When Krukenberg reached Hasenheide, which was the rendezvous point for the division, he went to meet with Ziegler. The two men had occasion to meet previously, in 1944 during the fighting in the Baltic States. He told Ziegler he was there to replace him. Ziegler was aware of this and cordially told Krukenberg that he might not hold the post for longer than 24 hours. According to Ziegler, defending Berlin was impossible and *"those higher-ups"* were made scapegoats. Krukenberg asked how many soldiers Ziegler had to man the front-line. He learned it was only around 70. The rest were too exhausted and needed rest. Shocked, Krukenberg didn't know what to say. Indeed, two regiments of panzer grenadiers the *'Nordland'* had could barely fill weak battalions. The formation had a few left-over tanks and some assault guns, but desperately needed fuel for both. The artillery regiment was a mere shadow of itself.

Soviet soldier during Berlin Battle, 1945.

German soldiers in a defensive position.

Danish *Sturmmann* of the *Danmark* Regiment in the *Nordland* Division.

The last Danish and Norwegian *Waffen-SS* volunteers served in this division, a few Swedes from the panzer reconnaissance battalion, some Fins and Swiss, but mostly the combat strength was complemented by native German citizens and the *Volksdeutschen* from Hungary and Romania. There was also a handful of Spaniards, led by *Waffen-Hauptsturmführer* Ezquerra, to complete this colourful mix[13].

Having familiarized himself with the situation, Krukenberg sent *SS-Untersturmführer* Patzak to bring over the French troops from the Olympic Stadium. Meanwhile, Pachur got busy reorganizing the command post.

Meanwhile, the French volunteers, packed tightly onto trucks, were making their way through Berlin, heading for Tempelhof. By this time, Berlin was awake and alive again, if you could say such a thing of a ruined city on the eve of the final Soviet assault. The city S-Bahn railroad was still functioning to some extent. In the streets and squares, people were eating sandwiches, and policemen directed traffic. Frenchmen started to sing: *"SS Marchiert im Feindesland, (SS marches in enemy land) Und singt ein Teufelslied*[14]*, (and sings a devil's song)".*

Soviet tank *T-34/85* accompanied by infantry, moves down the street on the outskirts of Berlin, April 1945.

German soldiers fighting in Berlin, April 1945.

A *Nordland* division vehicle destroyed by bombing in a Berlin street, April 1945.

The surprised Berliners were watching the SS-men from their windows, and greeted and applauded them. Many probably thought they were the spearhead of Wenck's army, which was to break through the encirclement and free the city, or so the official propaganda claimed. Optimism, if somewhat false, was alive in Berlin. Teary-eyed, the French reciprocated the warm welcome they received. They waved their guns around and blew kisses to women. As the trucks came to a halt, they were quickly surrounded by a thick throng of people. The volunteers did not have much to give the civilians, other than cigarettes. Berliners could return only smiles and words of comfort. Soon they were on their way again, having shaken hands and expressed appreciation for the kindness they were shown. By late afternoon, the French SS-Assault Battalion arrived in the Neukölln sector in the south-east of the city and found quarters north of Hasenheide, between Hermannplatz and the church on Gardepionierplatz. The men made their lodgings in nearby pubs, one of which was still quite well-`stocked with beer, and in a carpet shop[15]. The Frenchmen noted that the city centre, having suffered around 360 air-strikes since 1940, was in abysmal shape. Streets were strewn with debris, pocketed with holes. On 21 March, the city officially stated that 26 km² of its surface was destroyed and a third of the houses were unsuitable for habitation[16]. All companies were ordered to send out scouting parties. One of those was led by *Waffen-Oberscharführer* Mongourd from the *2.Kompanie*. He took his platoon with him, 20-men strong. Although many of those, given their young age, had yet to see battle, they were all eager for a fight. At the head of the platoon walked Jean-Francois Lapland, who wasn't even 18, and his team leader, *Waffen-Unterscharführer* Fodot. The sun was slowly setting and the streets were emptying.

Members of the Hitler Youth in the defense of Berlin, April 1945.

A German concealed anti-tank gun, Berlin 1945.

Soviet troops in Berlin, April 1945.

Lapland could hear the rattle of a machine-gun and missile blasts, but couldn't pin down their location. He was aware, however, that the Russians were close. Suddenly, they heard fire very close by. They all hugged a wall. Moments later, Lapland and Fodot saw they were alone where had the others gone? They heard quiet voices. Speaking Russian! They quickly jumped into a hole behind the fence around one of the buildings. Soon, they saw two tanks, curiously without infantry support. They decided to wait and see what was to happen next. Around 3:00 a.m., they left their hiding place and approached the tanks. The only sound breaking the silence was a low hum of the radio. It seemed that the Soviets were either asleep or passed out drunk. The two Frenchmen made a quick decision. They took their panzerfausts, aimed and fired. Both tanks were set ablaze in a roar of fire. Later on, the pair were able to find their platoon. *Waffen-Oscha.* Mongourd told them that at dawn in just a few hours the counter-attack was to commence and that they were to take part. Their battle was to begin. Meanwhile, Gustav Krukenberg's priority was to move the command post away from Hasenheide, as the building it was previously in was no longer usable after the bombardment it had suffered. He decided to move it to the barracks in Gneisenau.

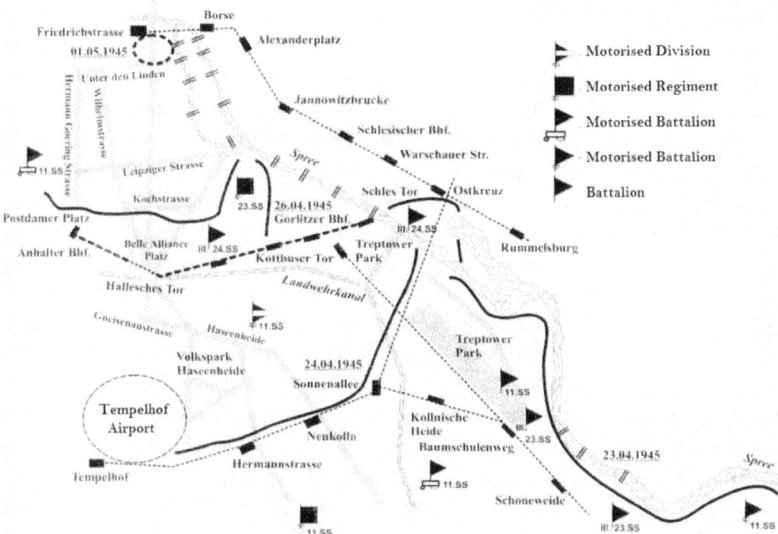

The operations of the *Nordland* Division in Berlin, April-May 1945.   German soldier.

A German soldier during Berlin fighting.

The barracks were nearby, so far completely untouched and, what was more important, they had excellent communications equipment. Once there, he sent a cable to Corps command (*LVI Panzer Corps*) asking to be assigned the defence of one of the sectors closer to the centre of the city. Having received a positive response, he ordered Division '*Nordland*' to the area near *Gendarmenmarkt*. As a result, Krukenberg chose the basement of the Berlin Opera House as his new Quarters[17]. He was then called to the Corps' staff and given written orders for the '*Nordland*' to take over the defence of sector Z[18] around noon the next day. The previous commander of this area was *Oberstleutnant* Seifert from the *Luftwaffe*, whose command post was located in the buildings of the Ministry of Aviation. Krukenberg went over there to speak with the man and take command. This did not go without trouble and a verbal skirmish, as Seifert did not have a good opinion of the *Waffen-SS*. His mistrust of the formation was deeply rooted. Having returned to his new quarters, around 11:00 p.m., Krukenberg was in a foul mood. Before turning in for the night, he gave orders to the commanding officers of the *Norge* and *Danmark* regiments. He was so troubled by Seifert's hostile attitude that he made the two officers aware of it. *SS-Brigadeführer* Gustav Krukenberg remembered the night of 25/26 April as quiet and calm. He did not know yet that the following nights would be anything but[19].

This article is an extract from the book "*The price of the oath: the French ss Sturmbataillon during the battle of Berlin 1945*", by Tomasz Borowski. The book is available directly from the author in e-book format. Price for complete book (250 pages main book + plus two colour sections and big Berlin map) is 7 GBP / 8 EUR. Paypal accepted.
For more info: tobor2@wp.pl.

Notes

(1) Jean Mabire, on p.113, writes "*just before midnight*", while Saint-Loup, on p 409, says "*at 3 am*".

(2) A commander and staff officer for the *Wehrmacht* during the Second World War. By the end of the war he was one of Hitler's closest advisors. On 29 April, along with Krebs, Joseph Goebbels and Martin Bormann, he witnessed Hitler's last will and he was one of its signatories. On the night of 1/2 May, after Hitler's and Goebbels' suicides, Burgdorf and Krebs took their lives as well.

(3) Today, it is difficult to ascertain to what extent Krukenberg believed these absurdities.

(4) Helmuth Weidling – German artillery officer in the Prussian army, Reichswehr and Wehrmacht (Wehrmacht Heer). Weidling was the last commander of the Berlin Area Defence during the Battle for Berlin. He defended the Third Reich capital from Soviet troops and finally gave the city up just before the end of the war in Europe.

(5) Forbes, Robert, op.cit.

(6) The name of the French *Waffen-SS* formation during the Battle for Berlin is often supplemented by '*Charlemagne*'. For example, Richard Landwehr uses the name '*SS-Sturmbataillon Charlemagne*' and Tony Le Tissier – SS '*Charlemagne*' Battalion. Interestingly, its commanding officer, Henri Fenet, does not use this title even once in his memoirs of the Battle for Berlin, A Berlin jusqu'au bout.

(7) Bouysse, Gregory, *Waffen-SS Français*, volume 1: officiers (Lulu Press, Inc., 2011).

(8) Weidling also had some *Waffen-SS* troops, commanded by *SS-Brigadeführer* Wilhelm Mohnke, who was charged with the defence of the government quarter on 22 April. In total, Weidling had only some 60,000 soldiers under his command, and only 50-60 tanks. LVI Panzer Corps and the *Waffen-SS* units were practically the only formations with adequate weaponry and any combat value to speak of.

(9) Tieke, Wilhelm, *Tragedy of the Faithful* (Fedorowicz Publishing, 2001), p.289.

(10) Beevor, Antony, *Berlin 1945*. Upadek (Znak, 2009), p.398.

(11) Steiner means *Nordland* Division.

(12) Steiner Felix, *Waffen SS Volunteers. Ideal and sacrifice* (Finna, 2010), p.242.

(13) Lefèvre, Eric, op.cit., p.18.

(14) The '*Waffen SS March*' could be considered something of an anthem for the formation, sung by soldiers of nearly all divisions. It was translated into Estonian, French and Norwegian, among others.

(15) Forbes, Robert, op.cit.

(16) Lefèvre, Eric, op.cit., p.18.

(17) The Staatsoper building, the State Opera House on Unter den Linden.

(18) According to the earlier order from Hitler, the city was divided into nine inner defence rings: sectors A and B (East Berlin), sector C (Neukolln), sector D (Tempelhof and Sterglitz), sector E (south-west Berlin and Grunewald), sector F (Spandau and Charlottenburg), sectors G and H (north Berlin) and sector Z (the city centre and the government quarter).

(19) Forbes, Robert, op.cit.

The First Italian Offensive in North Africa
by Ralph Riccio

Italo Balbo and General Tellera in Libya, 1940.

Italian colonial troops in Libya, 1940.

CV-33 **light tanks in Cyrenaica.**

Operazione "E"
(13 - 16 September 1940)

The Italian military situation in North Africa became more favorable following the defeat of France by the Axis, as the demilitarization of French forces in Tunisia allowed the bulk of Italian troops in Libya to be shifted to the Egyptian border. The conquest of Egypt and the Suez Canal would have allowed Italy to link up its colonies in North Africa and East Africa and to eliminate British Royal Navy support facilities in the Mediterranean. In North Africa the governor of Libya, Italo Balbo, had the Fifth Army under General Italo Gariboldi and the Tenth Army under General Mario Berti.

The Fifth Army under Gariboldi, with 500 artillery pieces and 2,200 trucks, consisted of three army corps:

X Corpo d'Armata under General Alberto Barbieri and consisting of the 25th Infantry Division *"Bologna"*, 55th Infantry Division *"Savona"* and 60th Infantry Division *"Sabratha"*;

XX Corpo d'Armata under General Cona with the 17th Infantry Divison *"Pavia"*, 27th Infantry Division *"Brescia"* and 62nd Infantry Divison *"Sirte"*;

XXIII Corpo d'Armata under General Bergonzoli, with the 1st Camicie Nere Division *"23 Marzo"*, 2nd Camicie Nere Division *"28 Ottobre"* and the 2nd Libyan Division.

The Tenth Army under General Berti, with about 200,000 men (plus 30,000

Libyan troops) had 339 L.3 light tanks organized into seven independent battalions, 1,600 artillery pieces and 1,000 trucks, and consisted of two army corps:

XXI Corpo d'Armata under General Lorenzo Dalmazzo with the 62nd Infantry Division *"Marmarica"* and 63rd Infantry Division *"Cirene"*;

XXII Corpo d'Armata under General Enrico Pitassi Mannella with the 64th Infantry Division *"Catanzaro"*, 4th Camicie Nere Division *"3 Gennaio"* and the 1st Libyan Division.

Annibale Bergonzoli.   **Sebastiano Gallina.**   **Generale Italo Gariboldi.**

Libyan Ascari of the Italian African Police.

Also available were the forces under General Sebastiano Gallina (Sahara Sector) divided into the *Comando Fronte Sud* (Southern Front Command) with two Libyan battalions, one machine gun company, 1 camel-borne battery with 65/17 guns and two 20mm heavy machine gun sections and the *Comando Truppe Sahara* (Sahara Troop Command) with one Saharian battalion, one motorized machine gun company, four *meharisti* companies and ten machine gun companies.

Italian camel-mounted troops, 1940.

In Egypt, the British had the *Western Desert Force* commanded by General Richard N. O'Connor, with about 36,000 men comprising the 7th Armoured Division, 4th Indian Division and 6th Australian Division. British equipment included 134 Mark VI light tanks, 114 cruiser medium tanks, a battalion of

Matilda infantry tanks and 38 armored cars. Aircraft numbers were the same as for the Italians. The British armored force worried Balbo who, aware of the superiority of the enemy tanks, urgently requested Rome for more powerful new medium tanks.

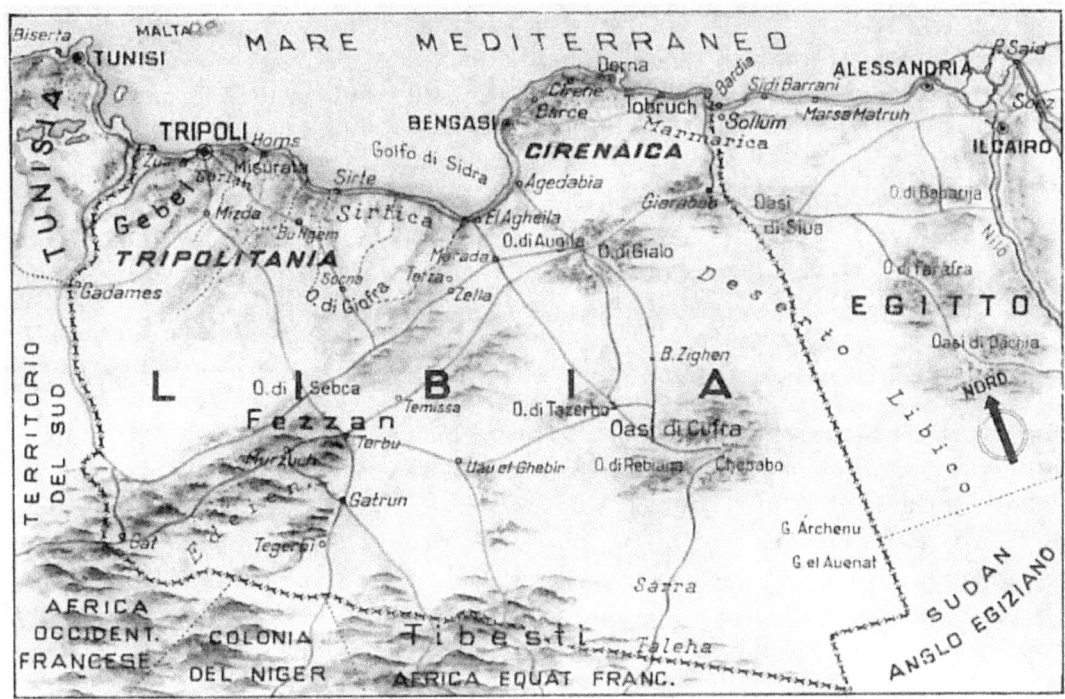

A late-1930s period postcard showing a map of Libya.

A *M11/39* medium tank during maneuvers.

Bersaglieri motorcycle troops, Libya 1940.

On June 20, the governor of Libya sent the following message to Marshal Badoglio:

"...Our assault tanks are old and armed only with old machine guns; the British machine guns mounted on their tanks have bullets that are able to penetrate the thin armor of our tanks. We have no tanks, the anti-tank guns are old and are not effective against the British tanks."

Following the defeat of France, the governor Italo Balbo had hoped to make up for the lack of supplies and equipment by collecting French materiel in Tunisia, but he was prevented from doing so by the terms of the Italo-French armistice.

He was able only to get a promise from Rome to send 70 M11/39 medium tanks by early July.

Initial Encounters

Following the declaration of war on June 10, 1940, it was the British who took the initiative and were the first to attack the Italian positions along the Libyan border. On July 11, armored cars of the 11th Hussars of the 7th Armoured Division crossed the border and attacked an Italian column escorted by 17 light tanks; all of the Italian tanks were destroyed or captured. During the fighting, Colonel Lorenzo D'Avanzo was killed, earning the first Gold Medal for Valor in North Africa.

Colonel Lorenzo D'Avanzo.

On 12 and 13 June, British attacks continued against isolated border posts at Ridotta Maddalena and Sidi Omar. Furthest to the north was Ridotta Capuzzo manned by about 200 soldiers, armed with three *Schwarzlose* machine guns; some 20 kilometers south of Capuzzo was Sidi Omar, with a garrison of about 60 soldiers. Still further to the south was Ridotta Maddalena, also with sagarrison of sixty men. The stronghold at Giarabub, with 800 men, two artillery pieces and 56 machine guns, was 150 kilometers south of Maddalena.

A *Rolls Royce* armoured car passing through Italian barbed wire on the Egyptian-Libyan frontier, July 1940.

British Light Tanks *MK VIB* of 7th Armoured Division in the desert.

Libyan soldiers lined up in front of Forte Capuzzo.

Between Giarabub and Maddalena were two platoons of Libyan ascaris, at Ueschechet el Heira and Garn el Grein. On June 14, the Italian units defending Ridotta Capuzzo were wiped out, while the *1º Raggruppamento Libico* (1st Libyan Group) had to abandon the positions at

Sidi Azeiz and pull back to Bardia. The Italians planned counteroffensive moves which, however, had no effect because the enemy units had themselves already withdrawn. On June 17, the outposts at Ueschechet and Garn el Grein were occupied by the British. Thus, in seven days all of the frontier posts along the Egyptian border fell to the British.

Savoia Marchetti SM79 flying over the Mediterranean.

An Italian coastal battery in Libya.

General Rodolfo Graziani.

It was not until 28 June, after signing the armistice with France, that the Italian high command decided to pass onto the offensive in Egypt; Badoglio sent Balbo a telegram to advise him to shift all available forces to the Egyptian border and to prepare for action by 15 July. However, on 28 June, at 1740 hours, an Italian S79 trimotor aircraft aboard which Balbo was approaching Tobruk from Derna was mistakenly shot down by anti-aircraft guns of the Italian cruiser *San Giorgio*. At the time an enemy air attack was under way over the city and the anti-aircraft gunners could not tell the Italian aircraft from the attacking British aircraft.

General Rodolfo Graziani took command of the Italian forces in North Africa; Graziani had previously been Governor of Tripolitania and had taken an active part in its reconquest following the First World War. Graziani arrived in Tripoli on 30 June. In early July, the 70 M11/39 medium tanks that had been promised to Balbo arrived, along with another 500 motor vehicles. The M11/39 medium tank had a 105 HP motor and was armed with a 37/40 gun and two Breda 8mm machine guns. The 70 M11/39 tanks were organized in two

Italian soldiers attacking, 1940.

battalions, the I and II, which were soon sent to the border with Egypt to challenge the British offensive raids that had continued to be carried out in July. On August 5, near Sidi Azeiz, the M11 medium tanks had their first encounter with British tanks and had the better of them; the British lost four tanks in the engagement.

A group of *M11/39* medium tanks marching in the Desert, summer 1940.

M11/39 advancing in the Egypt, summer 1940.

On August 29, the I and II battalions wer integrated into the newly formed *Comando carri armati della Libia*, which consisted of of two *raggruppamenti*, each with three light tank (L3/35) tank battalions and one medium (M11/39) battalion. The *1º raggruppamento carri* was commanded by Colonel Pietro Aresca, being assigned to the XXIII Army Corps and the *2º raggruppamento carri* by Colonel Antonio Trivioli being assigned to the Group of Libyan Divisions. In addition, a mixed tank battalion was formed consisting of one company each of L3/35 and M11/39 tanks, assigned to the *Raggruppamento Maletti*.

The Offensive Begins

At the end of August, after several arguments between Mussolini and Badoglio, Graziani began to plan an Italian offensive against Egypt. The plan called for an advance on Sidi Barrani along two axes, one in the north along the coast and one in the south along the Bir er Rabia-Bir er Enba track.

Italian infantry advancing further into the desert.

General Pietro Maletti.

A Motorised column of the *Raggruppamento Maletti* moving towards Sidi Barrani, 1940.

In order to carry all of the troops with the available trucks, it was decided to limit the forces to be employed in the offensive to five divisions, plus the Special Group under General Pietro Maletti. The three divisions of General Bergonzoli's XXIII Army Corps were to advance along the coast road, while to the south the two Libyan divisions under General Gallina would make their advance. The *Raggruppamento Maletti*, completely motorized and with a wide radius of action, was to remain in reserve. Graziani requested 600 trucks from Rome in order to completely motorize the attack force. At 15:30 on September 7, 1940, Mussolini ordered that the offensive should begin on 9 September, without the trucks that had been requested.

Sidi Barrani

Unable to transport all of the units by truck, Graziani had to modify his plans for the offensive, leading to the decision to have the bulk of the troops advance along the coast road. On September 8, orders were issued for the advance: the Group of Libyan Divisions would take the lead, followed by the XXIII Army Corps. The '*23 Marzo*' Camicie Nere division under General Antonelli was kept in reserve, while the *Raggruppamento Maletti* was to be ready for any move on the flank of the British deployment. To support the ground troops Graziani could count on the 5th Squadra Aerea of Libya, with 300 aircraft. From the beginning, the advance of the Italian troops in Egyptian territory was hampered by bad weather.

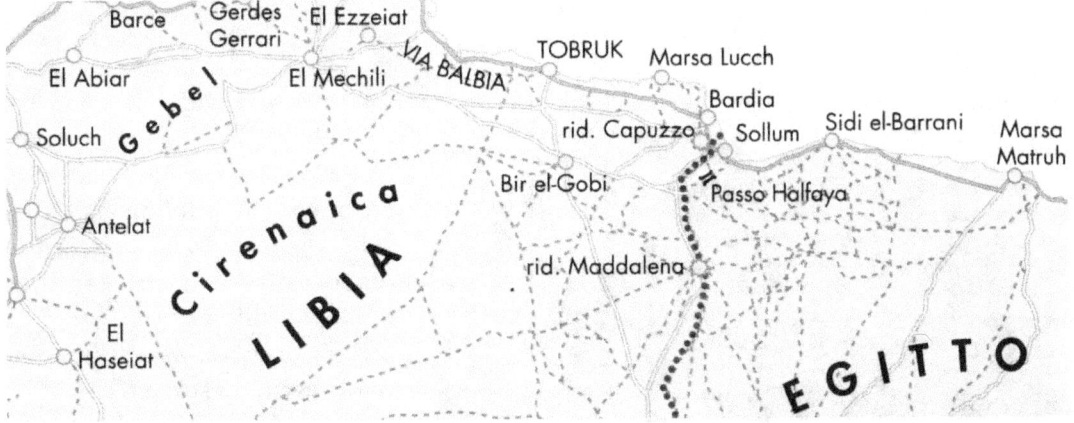

A ghibli arose, reducing visibility as well as air support, and the temperature was 45 degrees Celsius (113 Fahrenheit) in the shade. The *Raggruppamento Maletti* advanced too far forward, and the XXIII Corps units also advanced too quickly, getting entangled with the Libyan divisions, creating chaos and overcrowding the coastal highway.

Blackshirts dragging a gun across the desert of Marmarica, Libya-Egypt, 1940.

Italian *M11/39* tanks heading to Sidi Barrani, 1940.

Blackshirts of the 4th Camicie Nere Division *'3 Gennaio'* on an armed truck in the Libyan desert in September 1940.

At dawn on September 12, Graziani was forced to call a 24-hour halt to straighten out the troop deployments. Some changes were also made to the invasion plans: the flanking move from the desert was abandoned, according priority to a frontal advance against Sidi Barrani. The attack towards Sollum, the first town across the border, began at dawn on Friday, 13 September, after a heavy artillery barrage and an air bombardment. By 0830 the 1st Libyan Division had occupied the outskirts of Sollum, forcing the British to withdraw, and the 2nd Libyan Division had taken Halfaya Pass. The advance resumed the following day, slowed down by strong British resistance who, thanks to their mobile artillery, were able to inflict heavy losses. The coast road was destroyed by the enemy who before falling back had enough time to lay several minefields. These actions caused further delays to the Italian advance; forced to avoid the main road, many Italian vehicles ended up bogging down on the sandy desert tracks or were damaged by mines. Despite all of these problems, at 1445 on 16 September the *"23 Marzo"* Camicie Nere made their entry into Sidi Barrani, which had by then been abandoned by the British. A series of reconnaissance patrols were made in all directions, without however finding any signs of the enemy. Italian losses during these first five days of fighting amounted to 120 killed and 410 wounded; a third of the losses were Libyans. The *Regia Aeronautica* lost six aircraft. The British claimed a loss of 50 men.

Italian troops advance on foot in the Libyan desert with light artillery in September 1940.

Italian light tanks L3 in the desert, September 1940.

Italian M11/39 tanks marching in the desert, 1940.

Mersa Matruh

With the fall of Sidi el Barrani, British forces dug in 120 kilometers further east, at Mersa Matruh. General O'Connor had planned to conduct a defensive battle with the few tanks that he had left, but for the moment, the British forces could not undertake any offensive action. But Graziani did not press his advance, and again asked Rome for more trucks to be able to continue the offensive. Instead of attacking the remaining British forces and destroying them, he busied himself with improving his supply lines and deployed his troops in a series of fortified camps. Between 7 and 8 October a flying column of the *"Cirene"* Division engaged a

British motorized column at Gabr bu Raydan. Once again Mussolini was forced to order Graziani to go on the offensive against Mersa Matruh between 10 and 15 October.

Trucks and soldiers of the Italian army advance in the desert of Sidi el Barrani, September 1940.

The new *M13/40* tanks began to arrive in October 1940.

Italian *Bersaglieri* fighting in the desert, 1940.

Graziani responded to the Duce by saying that he would not be ready until the end of October; in order to attack the fortified positions at Mersa Matruh he needed two groups of artillery with 149/13 guns, trucks to move the units and trailers to tow the new M13/40 medium tanks that had arrived in Africa. In early October, 37 M13/40 medium tanks had arrived in North Africa; these tanks were superior to the M.11 tanks and were equipped with a 47/32 gun and four Breda 8mm machine guns. The M.13s were all assigned to the III Tank Battalion.

With the beginning of the Greek campaign (28 October 1940), Graziani lost all hope of receiving the reinforcements he had requested and began to plan an attack against Mersa Matruh with the forces he had available to him. The British, in the face of Italian passivity (except for a brief clash on 5 November east of Maktila) resumed harassing attacks against the Italian outposts.

A column of *M11/39* tanks advancing in the desert.

On the night of November 18, enemy armored vehicles infiltrated the Italian defensive positions around Sidi el Barrani. In order to throw them back, the medium tank battalion of the I Armored Group, a flying column of the 2ⁿᵈ Libyan Division and a column from the *Raggruppamento Maletti* had to be called into action. The following day, the two Italian columns pushed back the British units, which however resumed their attack soon after, hitting the Italian units while they were withdrawing. Rearguard actions ensued which were resolved by the Italian air force which strafed the British forces, forcing them to retire. At the same time a group of Italian CR.42 fighter planes faced off against an enemy air squadron, downing six planes without incurring any losses. The Italian units remained at Sidi Barrani until December, despite an avalanche of telegrams by Mussolini to Graziani urging him to resume the offensive. In one of the dispatches the Duce was most eloquent about the wait-and-see attitude of the commander of troops in Africa: *"Who benefited most from this long pause, us or the enemy? I don't hesitate even a moment to answer that, it has benefited the enemy not only more but also exclusively"*. In fact the British had all the time they needed to reorganize and to prepare for a counteroffensive against the Italian forces in early December. On November 25, the *Comando carri armati della Libia* became the *Brigata corazzata speciale*, commonly referred to as the *Brigata corazzata speciale Babini*, named after its commander, General Valentino Babini, in order to operationally group together all of the various separate tank units present in the theater. Its aim was to constitute a formation that was sufficiently mobile and powerful enough to challenge the British mechanized units of the *Western Desert Force*. The brigade was much larger than its predecessor and included the 10ᵗʰ Bersaglieri Regiment, a motorcycle battalion, a tank command with a tank regiment with one light and two medium tank battalions, a mixed tank regiment with one light tank battalion and one medium battalion with the newly arrived M13/40 tanks, an artillery regiment and service and support troops. The XXI light tank battalion had transitioned to the newly arrived M 13/40 medium tanks, but the crews had virtually no time to acclimate themselves to the new machines, with predictable negative results when later engaged in combat. The brigade's structure fluctuated and varied with the addition and removal of various units up to battalion size between the time of its inception and its combat engagement in early December 1940. In February 1941, at Beda Fomm the brigade, then consisting of one *M13/40* medium tank battalion, a light tank battalion and an artillery regiment, fought desperately but in a rather uncoordinated fashion and was essentially wiped out.

Bibliography

F. Bandini, *"Gli italiani in Africa"*, Mondadori editore

A. Bongiovanni, *"Battaglie nel deserto"*, Mursia editore

M. Montanari, *"Le operazioni in Africa settentrionale"*, Ufficio Storico S.M.E.

WW2 AXIS
FORCES